The Christian & Calvinism

A critical examination of Calvinism's Five Points, namely, (1) Total Depravity, (2) Unconditional Election, (3) Limited Atonement, (4) Irresistible Grace, and (5) the Perseverance of the Saints, with accompanying thoughts on the impact these have had on the thinking of far too many Christians

Allan Turner

The Christian & Calvinism

Published by Allanita Press

Cover design by Steve Sebree, Moonlight Graphics
Printed in the United States of America

ISBN 0-9777350-3-6

For information:
Allanita Press Publishing
585 Cox Road
Roswell, Georgia 30075

Dedication

This book is dedicated to the memory of Gregory Lynn "Greg" Steele, who was, and no doubt remains, one of the sweet singers of Israel. In addition to being my friend, brother in Christ, and a fellow soldier of the Cross, he demonstrated himself to be a faithful and generous supporter of both my preaching and my writing. He was a great encouragement to me over the years. His long struggle with the disease that ravished his body and ultimately took his life was, I can confidently say, extraordinarily valiant. Although Greg wanted to live, he was prepared to die. And he died as he had lived, trusting in the magnificent and glorious promises of Almighty God.*

*"For I am persuaded that neither death nor life, nor angels nor principalities nor powers, nor things present nor things to come, nor height nor depth, nor any other created thing, shall be able to separate us from the love of God which is in Christ Jesus our Lord."

—*Romans 8:38-39*

Table of Contents

Chapter 1

Introduction

John Calvin, the brilliant systematic theologian of the Reformation, in explaining predestination, said:

> *Predestination we call the eternal decree of God, by which He has determined in Himself, what would have to become of every individual of mankind. For they are not all created with a similar destiny; but eternal life is foreordained for some and eternal death for others. Every man, therefore, being created for one or the other of these ends, we say he is predestinated either to life or to death.*[1]

According to Loraine Boettner, the well-known interpreter of Calvinism, Martin Luther, the father of the Reformation, "was as zealous for absolute predestination as was Calvin."[2] To prove his point, Boettner quotes Luther's commentary on Romans, where Luther said:

> *All things whatever arise from, and depend on, the divine appointment; whereby it was foreordained who should receive the word of life, and who should disbelieve it; who should be delivered from their sins, and who should be hardened in them; and who should be justified and who should be condemned.*

---

[1] *Institutes of the Christian Religion*, Book III, Chapter XXI, section 5.

[2] *The Reformed Doctrine of Predestination*, page 15.

To further make his point, Boettner even quotes Melanchthon, Calvin's student, who is reported to have said: "All things turn out according to divine predestination; not only the works we do outwardly, but even the thoughts we think inwardly"; and again, "There is no such thing as chance, or fortune; nor is there a readier way to gain the fear of God...than to be thoroughly versed in the doctrine of Predestination." Furthermore, Benjamin B. Warfield, who, in the opinion of some Calvinists, is the most outstanding Reformed theologian since Calvin himself, makes his belief in absolute predestination very clear. In an article entitled "Predestination," Warfield said that Predestination was "broad enough to embrace the whole universe of things, and minute enough to concern itself with the smallest details, and actualizing itself with inevitable certainty in every event that comes to pass."[3]

What Calvinists Teach Is Clear

Calvinists believe that absolutely nothing happens that God has not foreordained or predestined to happen! If an individual goes to heaven, it is because God predestined that he would, independent of anything this individual would do of his own free will; on the other hand, if an individual goes to hell, it is because God predestined that he would, independent of anything this individual would do of his own free will. This point is clearly stated in the *Westminster Confession*:

> *Those of mankind that are predestinated unto life, God, before the foundation of the world was laid, according to His eternal and immutable purpose, and the secret counsel and good*

---

[3] *Biblical Doctrines*, pages 13, 22.

pleasure of His will, hath chosen in Christ, unto everlasting glory, out of His mere grace and love, without any foresight of faith or good works, or perseverance in either of them, or any other thing in the creature, as conditions, or causes moving Him thereunto; and all to the praise of His glorious grace."[4]

It is against such error that this study is dedicated.

What I Believe The Bible Teaches

I believe the Bible teaches that Christ died for all people, for those who perish no less than for those who are saved; that the election of the saints is not an unconditional act of God; that saving grace is actually extended to every man, which he may then receive or reject; that man may resist the Holy Spirit's invitation to be saved, if he so chooses; that God's grace, once accepted, can then be rejected and is, therefore, not necessarily permanent, but that those who are ransomed by the precious blood of Christ can, if they are so disposed, throw away all God has so graciously given them and perish eternally.

This statement is not a creed to be implemented in all the churches; it is, instead, my own systematic theology. It is my conviction that all these things are taught in the Bible. I stand ready to give a reason for the hope that is in me by citing book, chapter, and verse for what I believe. Actually, the design of this study is to do exactly this! As I examine the cardinal arguments (points) of Calvinism, I will be refuting each argument the Calvinists make with a "thus sayeth the Lord." This is only as it should be, for the final

---

[4] Chapter III, sections III-VII.

authority by which any doctrine or theological system is to be judged must always be God's word.

When it comes to Calvinism, many Christians continue to be "children, tossed to and fro and carried about with every wind of doctrine, by the trickery of men, in the cunning craftiness by which they lie in wait to deceive."[5] This is not because the Bible is somehow unclear on the subject. In point of fact, the Bible clearly and emphatically denies Calvinism. If God is "not willing that any should perish, but that all should come to repentance,"[6] *then Calvinism simply cannot be true.*

The problem for many is that the Bible is not a book on systematic theology. For example, the Bible teaches, but does not systematically set forth, the doctrines of the triune nature of God, the deity of Christ, the personality of the Holy Spirit, the reality of future rewards in heaven and condemnation in hell, all of which are questioned by some who claim to be Christians.

Nevertheless, the Bible is God's special revelation to man. As such, it has a beginning and an end. When one has studied this revelation from beginning to end, he then knows what it is God wants him to know about the myriad subjects contained therein. Only then can one begin to systematize these subjects.

Although systematization is an essential process of theology,[7] it is at this very point that men begin to go astray. This problem is dealt with by the apostle Paul, who said, "Study to shew thyself approved unto God, a workman that needeth not to be ashamed, rightly dividing the word of truth."[8]

---

[5] Ephesians 4:14.

[6] 2 Peter 3:9.

[7] By theology we mean only the legitimate study of God and His revelation.

[8] 2 Timothy 2:15, KJV.

God's word always accomplishes what He intends; in other words, it never returns void.[9] Therefore, how we interpret or "rightly divide" the Scriptures is extremely important. It is at this point that sheep begin to be separated from goats.[10] There is no excuse for getting caught up in the error of Calvinism, none except ignorance of God's word!

Unfortunately, ignorance is a major problem among God's people today. Some are ignorant because they are still babes in Christ. Others are ignorant because they lack someone to teach them. Still, other Christians are ignorant through no fault but their own. They do not like to study God's word. Studying is hard work. It requires one to think and, quite frankly, these folks just do not want to think. However, if we are not ready to study the word of God, *thinking it out* and *thinking it through*, then we will, quite naturally, wrest the Scriptures to our own destruction.[11]

So, if you are not willing to "gird up the loins of your mind,"[12] then this book is not for you. Consequently, your lot in this life is to be "tossed to and fro, and carried about with every wind of doctrine, by the sleight of men, and cunning craftiness, whereby they lie in wait to deceive."[13] On the other hand, if you, like a new born babe, "desire the pure milk of the word, that you may grow thereby,"[14] then I believe you will appreciate this study.

Always keep in mind that this study represents the thinking of the author, who has endeavored to "speak as the oracles of God."[15]

---

9 Isaiah 55:11.
10 John 10:16,27; Revelation 3:20.
11 See 2 Peter 3:16.
12 1 Peter 1:13.
13 Ephesians 4:14, KJV.
14 2 Peter 2:2.
15 1 Peter 4:11.

He could be wrong! Ultimately, it is your responsibility to "search the Scriptures" for yourself[16] to see whether these things are so.[17] The author has cited passages he believes authenticate his arguments. As you engage in this study, please read these passages for yourself. Make sure they are used correctly and not taken out of context. May God richly bless you as you study His word.

16 John 5:39.
17 See Acts 17:11.

Chapter 2

God's Sovereignty

In an over-reaction to Calvinist extremes, many Christians have shied away from a study of God's sovereignty. This is a serious mistake. The sovereignty of God is a thoroughly biblical subject. Although the words "sovereign" or "sovereignty" are not found in the KJV, one or both of these words appear in the NKJV, ASV, NIV, and NRSV. Nevertheless, the idea of God's sovereignty is clearly taught in both the Old and New Testaments. "Sovereignty," according to the *American Heritage Dictionary*, means, "Supremacy of authority or rule as exercised by a sovereign." This idea is applied to God by such words as "dominion," "rule," "ruler," "Lord," "King," and "Potentate." As Jack Cottrell points out in his outstanding book, *What The Bible Says About God The Ruler*, "The sovereignty of God may be concisely summed up as absolute Lordship." Sovereignty, then, is equal to lordship, lordship is equal to ownership, and ownership is equal to control. *It is precisely at this point that Calvinism strays.* We will have more to say about this farther along; but before proceeding on, let us make sure we understand the ramifications of Sovereignty.

The Ramifications Of Sovereignty

If God is truly the Sovereign of the universe, then whatever happens, we are told, is the will of God. A young baby dies of cancer or a young mother or father is seriously injured in an automobile accident and this is said to be God's will. We pray earnestly for a fellow Christian's recovery from a serious illness and in closing our prayer we say, "Not our will but Thine be done." But, recovery does not take place and death occurs. Has God's will really been done? Invariably, at funerals, if one listens to what is being said to the bereaved, one will be heard saying, "It is God's will." Are these things truly God's will, and if so, in what sense?

Repelled by the thought of a loving God being responsible for the death of the innocent and those we love, many Christians have concluded that God is not yet Sovereign Ruler of the universe. Unlike now, one day, they say, God's will is to be done in all things. As sympathetic as I am to their reasons for coming to this conclusion, I am nevertheless convinced that those who hold such a position are terribly wrong. From a biblical standpoint, the sovereignty of God is simply not open for debate. If God is not sovereign, He is clearly not God! Therefore, when I answer "yes" to the question, *"Is it true that whatever happens is the will of God?,"* I must make sure that those who hear me understand that my answer is not an *unqualified* "yes." Failing to do so would be theologically misleading and personally devastating.

My "yes" is qualified by the fact that there are at least three different senses in which the "will of God" is used in the Bible. When we understand the different ways in which this phrase is used, then we can understand that God is not personally nor directly responsible for the many things people want to either credit or discredit Him with, even though it remains true that everything that happens ultimately falls within His sovereignty.

God's Decretive Will

There are things that God decrees to happen. He causes these things to happen by His own omnipotence. These can be described as God's decretive or decreed will. A biblical description of God's decretive will is found in Psalm 33:11, which says: "The counsel of the Lord stands forever, the plans of His heart from generation to generation," and again in Isaiah 14:27, which says: "For the Lord of hosts has planned, and who can frustrate it? And as for His stretched-out hand, who can turn it back?" It was God's decretive will that was at work in His scheme to redeem mankind through His Son Jesus Christ.[1] For the Bible believer, it is a given that whatever God purposes cannot be frustrated.

For example, in Romans 8:28-30, we learn that God has decreed that He will justify, and one day glorify, certain foreknown individuals (viz., "whosoever will") on the basis of a foreordained Christ,[2] a foreordained gospel plan,[3] and a foreordained life.[4] With this fact firmly established, the apostle Paul joyously affirms, "If God is for us, who can be against us?"[5] Amen, and amen!

In like manner, the doctrine of the resurrection rests firmly on God's decretive will. In John 6:40, Jesus said, "And this is the will of Him who sent Me, that everyone who sees the Son and believes in Him may have everlasting life; and I will raise him up at the last day." Again, "If God is for us, who can be against us?" *Whatever God proposes, and Himself carries out, will, in fact, happen.* This is the reason why God can assert that He declares "the end from the beginning, and from ancient times things that are not yet done, saying, 'My counsel shall stand, and I will do all My pleasure.'"[6] This is God's decretive will.

---

1 Acts 2:23; 4:28; Colossians 1:4.
2 Acts 2:23; 1 Peter 1:19, 20.
3 Acts 2:23; 1 Peter 1:19, 20.
4 Ephesians 2:10.
5 Romans 8:31.
6 Isaiah 46:10.

God's Preceptive Will

But there is a second way in which the "will of God" is used in the Bible. This has to do not with what God purposed to do Himself, but with what He desires for man to do. *This can be described as God's preceptive will and is primarily concerned with man's obedience to His word or precepts.* The writer of Hebrews speaks of the "will of God" in this sense when he writes, "For you have need of endurance, so that after you have done the will of God, you may receive the promise."[7] It was in this sense that the Lord used the expression in Matthew 7:21: "Not everyone who says to Me, Lord, Lord, shall enter the kingdom of heaven, but he who does the will of My Father in heaven." When Jesus said "the will of My Father," He was speaking of God's precepts, statutes, or commandments. Consequently, it is in connection with God's preceptive will, and not His decretive will, that man is commanded to "work out [his] own salvation with fear and trembling."[8]

Furthermore, it is in connection with God's preceptive will that we understand that the Lord is "longsuffering toward us, not willing that any should perish but that all should come to repentance."[9] Actually, God's desire (i.e., His will) for the salvation of all men is reflected many places in His word,[10] but such must be kept distinct from His decretive will. A failure to make such a distinction will cause one to land squarely within the Calvinist camp.

---

7 Hebrews 10:36.
8 Philippians 2:12.
9 2 Peter 3:9.
10 See 1 Timothy 2:4; Luke 7:30; Matthew 23:37.

God's Permissive Will

There is a third sense in which the "will of God" is used in the Scriptures. It can be described as God's permissive will. Perhaps it is with God's permissive will that men have the most trouble. *In this category are to be found all those things which God neither purposes nor desires, but which He allows man, in his freedom, to bring about.*[11] That which makes this third category different from the second is not the presence of God's permission, but the absence of a stated desire on God's part that these events or circumstances should happen. In this category are events God neither purposed nor desired, but, nevertheless, permits, including some things that are clearly contrary to His stated desire (will), such as man's sins. Therefore, in Jeremiah 19:5, when God said, "They have also built the high places of Baal, to burn their sons with fire for burnt offerings to Baal, which I did not command or speak, nor did it come into my mind," He made it plain that it was not His will they were doing, whether decretive or preceptive. In other words, it was not the mind (will) of God that they should do such a thing. Nevertheless, the Lord permitted His people to exercise their free wills and do those things clearly contrary to His counsel (will). Things such as this are within the "will of God" only in the sense that He permits them to happen.[12]

---

11 There is a sense in which this third category is related to the second, God's preceptive will. With a strict use of the word "permissive," it can be seen that man's response to God's desire or preceptive will is not decreed or purposed by Him, and is, therefore, permitted. In other words, God does not make someone obey His laws; but, in the strictest sense, He simply permits one to do so.

12 See Acts 17:24-30; 14:16; Romans 1:18-32.

God's permissive will allows both bad and good things to occur. It is used by Paul in this latter sense in 1 Corinthians 16:7, when he writes: "For I do not wish to see you now on the way; but I hope to stay a while with you, if the Lord permits." Again, he uses it this way when, in Acts 18:21, he writes: "I must by all means keep this coming feast in Jerusalem; but I will return again to you, God willing." The writer of Hebrews put it this way: "And this we will do if God permits."[13]

Of course, sometimes the Lord does not will (permit) something to happen that His creatures desire to happen. As Sovereign, He has the perfect right to do so. For example, in Acts 16:7, Luke writes: "After they had come to Mysia they tried to go into Bithynia, but the Spirit did not permit them." And, according to James, the height of man's prideful arrogance is manifested by the one who does not take into consideration the fact that his desires may be, and sometimes are, superseded by the Sovereign Ruler of the universe.[14]

Control Not Causation

Calvinists have thought that the key to sovereignty is causation. They are wrong. *The key to sovereignty is ultimate control.* Through His absolute foreknowledge of every plan of man's heart, and through His absolute ability (omnipotence) to either permit or prevent any particular plan man may have, God maintains complete control (sovereignty) over His creation. The power to prevent means that God ultimately has the final word in everything that happens. To deny this is to deny the sovereignty of God!

---

13 Hebrews 6:3.

14 See James 4:13-15.

It is true, then, that whatever happens is God's will. Everything that transpires falls within the sovereign will of God in one sense or another. However, it is absolutely crucial to understand that there are three different senses in which this may be true: (1) Sometimes a thing occurs because God decides it will happen, and then He makes it happen. This we have called *God's decretive will* and it seems to be limited mostly to His working out the "scheme of redemption." (2) Sometimes a thing occurs because God desires it and man decides, of his own free will, to do what God desires. This we have identified as *God's preceptive will* and has to do with God's commandments or precepts. (3) Sometimes a thing occurs because of the agency of an individual or group of individuals, and God permits it to happen. We have called this *God's permissive will.* Included in this category are sinful or careless acts like murder, or the death of one caused by the actions of a drunken driver. Even tragedies that occur through the natural processes would fit in this category. All three of these categories can be classified as "God's will," but only the first category is God's will in any causative sense. And even though God is Sovereign Ruler of the universe, categories two and three remind us that we must allow the Sovereign Ruler to respect the integrity of the freedom He has so graciously accorded His creation. As His creatures, we must learn to trust God's wisdom in knowing what good can be drawn from the tragic episodes He permits to take place in category three.

Does God Have An Individual Will For Each Person's Life?

Those who ask this question assume an individual, specific will for every person. They assume that God has an ideal, detailed blueprint already drawn up for each person's life. They assume that for any decision we face there is a specific choice (in the most restrictive sense) that God wants us to make. This applies to the school we should attend, the occupation we should choose, and the specific individual God wants us to marry. In his book, *Knowing God's Will, And Doing It!*, J. Grant Howard, Jr. expressed it this way:

> *Scripture teaches us that God has a predetermined plan for every life. It is that which will happen. It is inevitable, unconditional, immutable, irresistible, comprehensive, and purposeful. It is also, for the most part, unpredictable. It includes everything, even sin and suffering. It involves everything, even human responsibility and human decisions.*[15]

A good summary of this view is given by Garry Friesen in his book, *Decision Making & the Will of God*:

> *God's individual will is that ideal, detailed life-plan which God has uniquely designed for each believer. This life-plan encompasses every decision we make and is the basis of God's daily guidance. This guidance is given through the indwelling Holy Spirit who progressively reveals God's life-plan to the heart of the individual believer....*[16]

Although this view is very popular, we are convinced that the idea of an individual, specific will of God for every detail of a person's life is not taught in God's word. Calvinists and other determinists argue that the Bible is filled with examples of individuals for whom God had a specific plan, such as Abraham, Isaac, Jacob, Moses, David, John the Baptist, Paul *et al*. But each of these examples was highly unusual and was related to God's working out of His plan of salvation for fallen mankind, that is, the Scheme

---

15 Page 12.
16 Page 35.

of Redemption. Furthermore, the specific plan that God had for each of these individuals was revealed to them by special revelation and, therefore, cannot be seen as normative for ordinary believers today.

Those who affirm God's individual will for each person usually cite passages like Psalm 32:8; Proverbs 3:5,6; Isaiah 30:20,21; Colossians 1:9 and 4:12; Romans 12:1,2; Ephesians 2:10 and 5:15-17. But when these passages are considered in their context, a much stronger case can be made for these passages in terms of God's preceptive or moral will (which we have already discussed at some length) and not His decretive will.

Being Led By The Spirit

But someone will say, "How about being 'led by the Spirit?'" In Romans 8:14, the Scriptures say, "For as many as are led by the Spirit of God, they are the sons of God," and in Galatians 5:18, it says, "But if you are led of the Spirit, you are not under law." The Calvinist thinks the Holy Spirit influences him through some mysterious inward guidance. The Bible does not teach such a doctrine, these two passages included, and we are firmly convinced that when one begins to listen to some inner voice, he is headed for trouble. In fact, Romans 8:26, 27 does not say anything about the Holy Spirit speaking to us at all. What it says is:

> *...the Spirit Himself makes intercession for us with groanings which cannot be uttered. Now He who searches the hearts knows what the mind of the Spirit is, because He makes intercession for the saints according to the will of God.*

Being led by the Spirit of God has to do with one's obedience to God's word (i.e., God's preceptive or moral will), which is, according to Ephesians 6:17, the "sword of the Spirit." Being led by the

Spirit in a direct way, like was promised to the apostles,[17] was never intended to be understood as being available to all Christians. In other words, direct guidance by God's Holy Spirit was promised specifically to the Lord's apostles, not Christians in general, and was for the specific purpose of revealing the Bible, not for inner guidance for all Christians.[18]

We find it ironic that those who are waiting to know God's will for themselves through some inner guidance or miracle apart from the Word are the very ones who miss God's will for their lives by not obeying His preceptive or moral will. I have personally taught the gospel to those caught up in this deceptive doctrine and have had them tell me that if God wanted them to be baptized for the remission of sins, He would have told them personally through a direct operation of the Holy Spirit. As they erroneously wait for a direct revelation of God's decretive will, they fail to obey His preceptive will. As one can see, this is a most damnable doctrine!

But, in rejecting such a doctrine, one must not jump to another equally extreme position which says that knowing the will of God is irrelevant to daily decision making. The will of God (particularly His preceptive will as revealed in the Scriptures) is always applicable to our daily lives. God's Word is to be the reference point for our decision making. This means that the most sophisticated technique for knowing the will of God in our lives is: "All Scripture is given by inspiration of God, and is profitable for doctrine, for reproof, for correction, for instruction in righteousness, that the man of God might be complete, thoroughly equipped for every good work."[19] This means that whatever God instructs us to do

---

17 John 16:12-14.

18 See Ephesians 3:3-5.

19 2 Timothy 3:16.

in His Word, either through commands or general principles, is His will for our lives. In other words, if God wants us to do it, then it is in the book! Thus, when the question is asked, "How can I know God's will for my life?," we answer, "Read the Bible."

Not As Many "Thou Shalts" And "Thou Shalt Nots" As You Might Think

Contrary to what a lot of people think, God's preceptive will for man has very few "thou shalts" and "thou shalt nots." Most of what God would have us do is learned from principles taught in His Word. This is why Bible study is so important. Unless we are thoroughly familiar with God's Word, we will not know the principles that allow us to make the right decisions in our lives. For example, when we are familiar with the sanctity of life ethic taught throughout the Bible, we are able to make the right decisions concerning the many pressing issues of our day, namely, abortion, euthanasia, capital punishment, *et cetera*. In times past, God's people perished because they were ignorant of His Word,[20] and the same thing can happen to us today if we are not careful.

But, and this is very important, many of the decisions we face every day are neither required nor forbidden. The key to understanding this point is to be found in the idea that it is not our task to know if a particular decision is God's will, but rather if it is within God's will. For example, the inspired apostle wrote, "But if anyone does not provide for his own, and especially for those of his household, he has denied the faith and is worse than an unbeliever."[21] This is God's preceptive will and it requires, among other

20 See Hosea 4:1.
21 1 Timothy 5:8.

things, that a parent provide nourishing food for his or her children. As long as this general principle is met, the specific decision of whether to have liver and onions or steak and green beans for dinner does not really matter. Whether one eats in the kitchen or the dining room, or whether the beans are fresh or frozen, or whether one has a hamburger for breakfast, lunch or dinner, does not matter to God. Once again, as long as the general requirements of this passage are being met, God is not really concerned about the specific choices that are made. Understanding this point can be liberating for those who have thought God wanted them to make a specific choice in every decision.

To be pleasing to God, everything we do must fall within His preceptive will,[22] even those things that are not specifically required by it, such as matters of opinion and indifference. For instance, we have the right (i.e., it falls within God's will) either to eat or not eat meat; but, and this is terribly important, we have no right to bind either of these on anyone else.[23] Likewise, we have the right (i.e., it falls within the umbrella of God's preceptive will) to send our children to either a public or private school; but we have no right to bind either of these on someone else. Furthermore, we have the right (i.e., God grants permission) to marry within or outside our own race; but we have no right to bind our personal convictions on another person. There are, of course, many other things that could be listed here, but you see the point, do you not?

God is not nearly as judgmental as some people think. When someone insists on making his personal convictions the judge and jury of other men's consciences, he becomes much more

---

22 See Colossians 3:17.

23 Romans 14:1-13.

judgmental than God Himself. The Bible teaches it is just as wrong to bind where God has not bound as it is to loose where He has not loosed. The apostle Paul warned against the former when he said, "Who are you to judge another man's servant?"[24]

Making Right Choices

Within the liberty we have in Christ, our desire is to make the best choice among the many different options we have been given. Unfortunately, our experiences tell us that we do not always make the best choices. After the fact, we realize that the exercising of an alternative option would have been a much better choice, although the choice we actually made was not sinful. Nevertheless, having seen how our choice turned out, we now know it was not the best choice. As we are often told, "Hindsight is better than foresight." What, then, is our problem? In truth, ours is a lack of wisdom!

The Bible says, "If any of you lacks wisdom, let him ask of God, who gives to all liberally and without reproach, and it will be given to him."[25] If the lack of wisdom is what keeps us from making the best choices, and it is, all we need to do is ask the Lord for wisdom and He'll give it to us. Then, we will always make the best choices in life—it's as simple as this! Or is it? Although this wisdom comes from God as a direct response to our prayer, and is, therefore, something other than just a knowledge of God's preceptive will, it must not be thought of as either a magic formula or instant omniscience. Neither should we think of it as something totally divorced from one's knowledge of the Scriptures. Yes, we are assured that if we ask the Lord for wisdom, He will give it to us,

---

[24] Romans 14:4.
[25] James 1:5.

but Proverbs 4:5 commands us to "Get wisdom, get understanding," implying that wisdom and understanding must be acquired and, consequently, not something to be received passively. Proverbs 4:5 qualifies James 1:5, that is, it tells us that wisdom is not going to be given without some effort on our part. Furthermore, wisdom has to do with how we use the knowledge we already have. Within the context of Proverbs 4, wisdom, which is identified as the "principle thing,"[26] is connected to "instruction," "doctrine," "commandments," being "taught," and by application to the subject at hand, a knowledge of God's word. In fact, even a casual reading of the "Wisdom Literature" will demonstrate the connection between instruction and wisdom.

In addition, Moses, at the beginning of the Law, said:

> *Surely I have taught you statutes and judgments, just as the Lord my God commanded me, that you should act according to them in the land which you go to possess. Therefore be careful to observe them; for this is your wisdom and your understanding in the sight of the peoples who will hear all these statutes, and say, "Surely this great nation is a wise and understanding people."*[27]

Again, wisdom and understanding are associated with God's instructions and commandments. In 2 Timothy 3:15, being "wise unto salvation" is connected with "the holy scriptures." Therefore, a man who is not studying to show himself approved[28] cannot be asking for wisdom "in faith, nothing wavering," as James 1:6 requires, and will not, therefore, be receiving anything from the Lord! Nevertheless, for those who desire and pray for wisdom,

---

26 Verse 7.

27 Deuteronomy 4:5-6.

28 2 Timothy 2:15.

willingly cultivating it with God's help, I have no doubt they will receive it.

In seeking wisdom, the following suggestions are offered:

- *Know as much about God as possible.* Proverbs 1:7 teaches, "The fear of the Lord is the beginning of knowledge, but fools despise wisdom and instruction." In Psalm 111:10, it is said, "The fear of the Lord is the beginning of wisdom; a good understanding have all those who do His commandments." Although the fear mentioned in these passages is not totally unaware of the "terror of the Lord,"[29] contextually, the word indicates reverence for and respectful awe of God's divine nature. What this means is that without reverence for and awe of God we cannot know what we ought to know and, further, we cannot ever hope to properly utilize the little knowledge we do have. For as long as I can remember, my regard for God has always moved me to think about His characteristics and attributes. Now, the more I have learned about Him, the more I have stood in awe and veneration of Him. In addition, the more I have learned about Him, the closer I have actually felt to Him. My fear of God has not just allowed me to know more about Him, it has actually allowed me to know Him, that is, to have an intimate, loving relationship with Him. As a result, loving God with all my heart, mind, soul, and strength has become the consuming passion of my life. I love Him more than my own wife, and I love her more than I do my own life. Consequently, I have never known greater love than His love for me and, as a direct result of His great love for

[29] See 2 Corinthians 5:11.

me, I have never loved more than I love Him. Although it at first seems ironic, as my "fear of God" (i.e., my reverence, veneration, and awe of God) has increased over the years, almost without me realizing it, my "fear" of Him has actually disappeared. How can this be? According to the apostle John: "There is no fear in love; but perfect love casts out fear, because fear involves torment. But he who fears has not been made perfect in love."[30] The relationship I now have with the heavenly Father, "in Christ," no longer involves the fear of torment. In Christ, I no longer have an adversarial relationship with God the Father. I am no longer antagonistic of His commandments, but joyfully and enthusiastically keep them from a heart filled with love.[31] All this has produced in me a careful "boldness."[32] Without the remission of my sins, which has been provided by the grace of God, and accomplished as a result of my faith in the blood of Christ, I would be absolutely terrified to go into the presence of the Lord.[33] But now, "in Christ," with the fear of His wrath having been taken away, I possess a boldness and confidence to enter into the very presence of God. I emphasize the idea of "careful boldness," because until I finish my course in this life, I could, through moral neglect, lose[34] that which God's faithfulness guarantees.[35] As I have had the opportunity to preach and teach God Almighty over the years, I have noticed this same effect produced in

---

30 1 John 4:18.
31 See John 14:15.
32 See Ephesians 3:12; Hebrews 10:19; 1 John 4:17.
33 See Hebrews 10:31; 2 Corinthians 5:11.
34 See Hebrews 3:6, 14.
35 See Philippians 1:6.

others. Truly, the fear of the Lord is the beginning of knowledge and wisdom. If, though, the only time we think about God is when we ask Him for wisdom, we might as well not waste our time. I remain confident that as we continue to learn more about God, our love for Him will only increase.

- *Know as much about God's word as possible.* Because knowledge is a requirement for wisdom, we should pray for wisdom while learning as much about God's word as possible. In other words, praying for wisdom is not a substitute for Bible study!

- *Know as much about life as possible.* This is a mighty big job, and one that, more often than not, comes with experience. The Hebrew writer makes this point when he says, "But solid food belongs to those who are of full age, that is, those who by reason of use have their senses exercised to discern both good and evil."[36] For example, if one did not know that most "birth control pills" actually prevent a fertilized egg from implanting on the wall of the mother's uterus, thereby receiving nourishment, it would be difficult to make a biblically informed proper decision about what method of birth control one might wish to use. Furthermore, unless one knew that *in vitro* fertilization routinely involved the destruction of fertilized ova, it would be almost impossible to make the right decision about this procedure. But, knowing about life is more than the accumulation of facts, it is also the cultivation of the knowledge of how these facts affect life. This is why respect for and consultation with our

[36] Hebrews 5:14.

elders is so important for one seeking wisdom.[37] Quite simply, they have seen more of life than we have and, therefore, should be wiser than we are.

- Finally, *know as much about wisdom as possible.* As we said previously, praying for wisdom does not result in instant omniscience. It is unfortunate that when many are faced with a decision, they say a prayer for wisdom; then, no matter what they decide, they assume that this particular decision was supplied by God. But, as we have indicated already, wisdom does not work this way. Wisdom is not specific answers to specific problems. Rather, wisdom is the ability to discern the best decision from those that are only better. We recognize that wisdom applies general knowledge and understanding to specific situations with excellent results. This means it is a skill! Consequently, as we pray for it, we realize it grows and increases with not just study, but the exercise of what we have studied and learned. Unfortunately, even a wise person sometimes makes a poor or even a bad decision. Nevertheless, trusting the Lord to give us wisdom, we continue to learn as much about God, His word, life in general, and wisdom as we can. Only in this manner will we become acquainted with and enlightened by true, worthwhile wisdom.

The Mistake Of Trying To Interpret Providence

The Christian has the assurance of God's special providence. This assurance compelled the apostle Paul to say, "And we know that all things work together for good to them that love God, to

[37] See Leviticus 19:32; Proverbs 16:31; 1 Peter 5:5.

them who are the called according to His purpose."[38] And again, "If God is for us, who can be against us?"[39] With this said, is it possible to know the will of God in and through circumstances that take place in this life? I believe the answer to this question is an emphatic "No!" When an event takes place, we have no way of knowing, short of actual inspiration, whether it falls within the decretive or permissive will of God. Previously, God's decretive will was described as that which God desires and Himself makes happen, and His permissive will as something which originates apart from His desire but that He permits because of man's free will, *et cetera*. In other words, an event can happen because God wants it to happen and causes it to happen, or it may happen for various other reasons. Consequently, *an event cannot communicate a message apart from special revelation*. Additionally, we have no way of knowing whether an event has taken place because of God's *general* providence, which encompasses all creation, or as a result of His *special* providence, which is directed toward the church of Christ exclusively.

As has already been noted, Calvinists erroneously believe that everything that happens is God's decretive or purposive will. Others, some of whom are Christians, believe they can actually interpret God's will (or providence) by events that take place in their lives, or the lives of others. For instance, a good man prospers and a bad man suffers hardship. Some are convinced that God is blessing the good man and punishing the bad man. *But is this really the case?* What happens when a good man suffers and a bad man prospers?

---

38 Romans 8:28.
39 Romans 8:31.

The Gamaliel Fallacy

If the book of Job teaches us anything, it is that circumstances or events, apart from revelation, cannot convey God's decretive will. Job was not suffering because he was an evil man, as his friends supposed; he was suffering because he was, in fact, a good man. Job's friends, and even Job himself, had fallen victim to what has come to be called the "Gamaliel fallacy," after the principle offered by the great Jewish teacher Gamaliel, who said:

> *And now I say to you, keep away from these men and let them alone; for if this plan or this work is of men, it will come to nothing; but if it is of God, you cannot overthrow it, lest you even be found to fight against God.*[40]

Although what Gamaliel said is ultimately true,[41] in actuality, it does not translate into very practical advice. One must keep in mind that this is Gamaliel's opinion and advice, not the Holy Spirit's. For instance, the Roman Catholic church, with its universal bishop (viz., the Pope or Papa Father), is an apostate church that has existed basically in its present form since A.D. 606. Does this mean that God is blessing Catholicism? Of course not! But, if you were to apply Gamaliel's advice to the Catholic church, you could not stand or fight against it spiritually. Likewise, there are many other false religions that seem to be enjoying great success, especially when measured by the world's standards. Does this mean that they, too, are being blessed by God? Again, the answer is obvious. *Worldly success is not necessarily a sign of God's blessings.* John the Baptist's ministry did not end in success according to the

---

[40] Acts 5:38, 39.

[41] Ultimately, in the end, God's cause will be vindicated.

world's standards, as he ended up in prison and eventually had his head cut off. But according to God's standards, he was completely successful. By man's standards, the ministries of the apostles were miserable failures. However, we know they were successful in God's sight. Therefore, from our limited and finite perspectives, we must accept Gamaliel's pronouncement as the fallacy it really is.

Is Private Speculation Necessarily Wrong?

Does this mean that it is inappropriate for a Christian to entertain his own private speculation about God's providential care, along with the various circumstances that seem to point in that direction? No, I do not believe this is wrong. But I do believe that, even in one's own private speculation, one must be very careful about thinking a certain event definitely means that God has done this or that, or even that He desires this or that to be done. This kind of carefulness was exhibited by Mordecai, who said to Esther, "Yet who knows whether you have come to the kingdom for such a time as this?"[42] Mordecai's statement must not be construed as a lack of faith in God's providential care for the Jews, for he advised Esther, in the same verse, that if she did not help, then "deliverance will arise for the Jews from another place." It seemed to Mordecai that Esther was in the right place at the right time, and that the hand of God might be providentially involved in her being queen; but without special revelation, he simply could not know for sure. Let us all learn to be as wise and trusting as Mordecai. Believing in the sovereignty of God, and based upon the promises God had

---

42 Esther 4:14.

made to His people, Mordecai was willing to trust God for deliverance, and so should we.

Undoubtedly, we can all recount the marvelous things that have happened to us in our lifetimes which we believe were providential. However, we should be careful not to cite these things as proof of God's special providence. Our proof is found in the promises contained in God's word. In the case of special providence, the apostle Paul declared by inspiration, "We know that all things work together for good to them that love God, to them that are called according to His purpose."[43] In other words, because of God's special providential care for us, every circumstance or event that happens to us will have either a good *purpose* or a good *result*, so long as we continue to love and obey Him. How do we know this? The Bible, God's preceptive will, tells us so! Consequently, our faith in God, the Sovereign Ruler of all creation, and His solemn promise that "all things work together for good to them that love God," relieve us of the burden of trying to figure out whether a particular event happened because of God's decretive or permissive will, and directs us to a thorough study of His preceptive will, which has been revealed to us in the Bible.

As we conclude this section on the sovereignty of God, let us think of Him as "the Lord, God Most High, the Possessor of heaven and earth."[44] Let us acknowledge that He "has established His throne in heaven, and His kingdom rules over all."[45] With the psalmist, let us say:

> *Bless the Lord, you His angels, who excel in strength, who do His word, heeding the voice of His word. Bless the Lord, all you His*

---

43 Romans 8:28.

44 Genesis 14:22.

45 Psalm 103:19.

hosts, you ministers of His, who do His pleasure. Bless the Lord, all His works, in all places of His dominion. Bless the Lord, O my soul![46]

[46] Psalm 103:20-22.

Chapter 3

Man's Free Will

Calvinists give lip-service to man's free will, but they do not really believe in it. They say that man, in order to have free will, needs only to voluntarily choose his acts in accord with his own desires and motives; it matters not that God, as Sovereign, has foreordained these desires and motives, along with the choices themselves. Now, does this sound like free moral agency to you?

According to Calvinists, a person may have only one course of action open to him and still be free. "For example," they say, "a man may be locked in a room, but not want to get out. He therefore cannot get out (that is certain), but equally he does not want to get out (he is not there against his will)."[1] In other words, even though God has foreordained every single choice one makes, every choice is still free because God has also foreordained that each choice man makes will be made voluntarily.

Carl F. H. Henry, the founding editor of *Christianity Today*, noted theologian, educator, lecturer, and author of more than twenty-five books, explains (?) it this way:

> *To be morally responsible man needs only the capacity for choice, not the freedom of contrary choice.... Human beings voluntarily choose to do what they do. The fact that God has*

---

1 D.A. Carson, *Divine Sovereignty And Human Responsibility*, page 207.

foreordained human choices and that His decree renders human actions certain does not therefore negate human choice.[2]

As the famed Calvinist Loraine Boettner asserts, "God so controls the thoughts and wills of men that they freely [?] and willingly [?] do what He has planned for them to do."[3] In an attempt to bolster his flawed theology, Boettner observes, "It is very noticeable, and in a sense it is reassuring to observe the fact, that the materialistic...philosophers deny as completely as do Calvinists this thing that is called free will."[4] How anyone who claims to believe in the Bible could feel reassured because materialistic philosophers had come to the same conclusion as he is absolutely shocking to me. It is apparent that although Calvinists are disposed to citing their "free will" shibboleths, they do not, for a moment, believe that man actually has free moral agency.

Man Possesses Free Will

There are myriad Bible passages that present the reception of God's blessing or cursing as contingent upon human choice. This is epitomized in Deuteronomy 11:26-28, which says: "Behold, I set before you today a blessing and a curse: the blessing, if you obey the commandments of the Lord your God which I command you today; and the curse, if you do not obey the commandments of the Lord your God, but turn aside from the way which I command you today, to go after other gods which you have not known." When Joshua challenged the people to "choose you this day whom

---

2 God, Revelation And Authority, VI:84, 85.
3 *Op. cit.*, page 222.
4 *Ibid.*

you will serve,"[5] he was addressing individuals who were free to make a moral decision. This is no place made clearer than in Matthew 23:37, where Jesus cried:

> *O Jerusalem, Jerusalem, the one who kills the prophets and stones those who are sent to her! How often I wanted to gather your children together, as a hen gathers her chicks under her wings, but you were not willing!*

Thus, the Bible teaches conclusively and emphatically that man has free will.

God's Will Can Be Rejected

As the passages cited above teach, not only does man possess free will, but he can actually exercise this free will in a way that defies God's will. In other words, although God is Sovereign Ruler, He does not always get everything He wants. To the Calvinists, such a statement is totally unthinkable and completely contrary to their concept of God's sovereignty. Even so, in Isaiah 65:12, God said, "Therefore I will number you for the sword, and you shall all bow down to the slaughter; because, when I called, you did not answer; when I spoke, you did not hear, but did evil before My eyes, and chose that in which I do not delight." Again, in 2 Peter 3:9, it is plainly stated that God is "not willing that any should perish but that all should come to repentance." If, as the Calvinists claim, God decrees everything that happens, and if, as the apostle Peter claims, God is not willing that any should perish, then all mankind will ultimately be saved. But even Calvinists reject the idea of Universalism. What, then, is their solution? Simply this: They must

[5] Joshua 24:15.

come to understand that Calvinism is not just anti-scriptural, which is certainly bad enough, but is anti-God as well. Calvin's god (with a little 'g') is not the God (with a big 'G') who has revealed Himself in the Bible. Calvin's god, apart from anything the creature may or may not do, predestines some to eternal life and others to eternal damnation. However, the God who has revealed Himself in the Bible actually pleads with His creatures to obey His preceptive will so they can be saved. This God, as opposed to Calvin's god, "desires all men to be saved and to come to the knowledge of the truth."[6]

Why Does God Permit Men To Reject His Will?

When men begin to say that God can force a man to freely do His will, they are talking meaningless nonsense. Citing a passage that says, "with God all things are possible,"[7] does not provide these folks any help. The "all things" that are possible with God are actually qualified by other scriptures and the law of non-contradiction. For example, the Bible says God cannot lie![8] Therefore, it is not possible for God to lie. This means that the "all things" that are possible with God must be those things consistent with His divine nature. Further, God cannot make 2 + 2 = 5. He cannot make it to be raining and not raining in the same place at the same time. He cannot give a hydrogen atom and a helium atom the same atomic structure. Finally, even God could not make man free and not free at the same time in the same way. In order for man to be free, God had to give him the opportunity to rebel.

---

6 1 Timothy 2:4.
7 Matthew 19:26.
8 Titus 1:2.

But there is much more to this story. In Psalm 32:1, David says, "Blessed is he whose transgression is forgiven, whose sin is covered." In verse 5, he continues: "I acknowledged my sin to You, and my iniquity I have not hidden. I said, 'I will confess my transgressions to the Lord,' and You forgave the iniquity of my sin." In verses 8-9, the Lord replies:

> *I will instruct you and teach you in the way you should go; I will guide you with My eye. Do not be like the horse or like the mule, which have no understanding, which must be harnessed with bit and bridle, else they will not come near you.*

Why did God allow David to sin? Why did He not simply stop David from sinning in the first place? The answer seems obvious: God did not want His servants to serve Him because they are forced to do so. He wants those who will serve Him to do so freely, willingly accepting His instructions and counsel. He wants a relationship with His creatures based on mutual affection and love, and not because of some kind of force.

The Almighty God, if He so desired, certainly had the power to bridle His creatures, forcefully manipulating their minds and hearts and turning them into robots (or mules), so that they are forced to do His will. But if He did this, He would not be able to achieve His purpose of developing free relationships—like the one He desired with David—with His creatures.

Indeed, He wants all men to repent and enter a free love-relationship with Himself. If He forced them to do this, as Calvinists allege, their allegiance could not be freely given, that is, they would no longer be men but mules. God, who made man in His own image, wants him to be conformed to the image of His Son.[9] Unless man is a free moral agent, this simply cannot be done!

What Man's Freedom Cost God

Man's free moral agency is a unique gift from God Almighty. Without it, we could not be what and who we are. No other earthly creature has been given this special freedom. Furthermore, it should almost go without saying that only God could have made a creature with free moral agency. Therefore, man's free will is a constant reminder of God's omnipotence. But for many, and this includes Calvinists, the opposite is true. As the secular philosopher J. L. Mackie says, "There is a fundamental difficulty in the notion of an omnipotent God creating men with free will, for if men's wills are really free this must mean that even God cannot control them, that is, that God is no longer omnipotent."[10] In his book, *The Inexhaustible God*, Royce Gruenler says that man's free will, which necessitates a future that is open and indefinite, is "logically incompatible with the doctrine of a sovereign God."[11] In other words, Calvinists believe that if man has free will, then God is actually impotent.

The fallacy in all this will be more completely exposed in the section to follow on foreknowledge. At this point, suffice it to say that it is God's foreknowledge which permits Him to maintain complete control of His world in spite of man's free will, because foreknowledge gives God the option of either permitting or preventing man's planned, free will choices, and as was pointed out in

---

9 See Romans 8:29.

10 "Evil and Omnipotence," *God and Evil: Reading in the Theological Problem of Evil*, ed. Nelson Pike, page 57.

11 Pages 43, 44.

the previous chapter on God's permissive will, *prevention is really the ultimate in control.*

Therefore, man's free will does not render God impotent. Nevertheless, it does, in fact, limit Him. But if God is really limited, then how can He continue to be omnipotent? Are not these two concepts mutually exclusive? *Only in the mind of the determinists!* As has already been pointed out, the "all things" that are possible with God are *qualified* by both Scripture and the law of non-contradiction. God can do all things *consistent* with His nature and that are not, in and of themselves, illogical. Therefore, if God, of His own free will, chooses to create creatures with free moral agency, and in order to do so, He must limit Himself, such self-limitations are not a denigration of His omnipotence, as the determinists think, but are, instead, a powerful demonstration of it, which is exactly the point I made at the beginning of this subsection.

In order to insure man's autonomy, God, of His own free will, was willing to pay a tremendous price. Although He did not have to do so, the Almighty God was willing to limit Himself in relation to His creation. This gives us some idea of just how important man is to God. Furthermore, and this ought to humble us greatly, the final measure of God's concern for man is to be found in the sacrifice of His only begotten Son. Praise God, the Sovereign Ruler, for His willingness to give us our freedom, even though it ultimately cost Him the sacrifice of His only begotten Son. "Alleluia! For the Lord God Omnipotent reigns!"[12]

---

12 Revelation 19:6.

Chapter 4

The Foreknowledge Of God

Psalm 147:5 says that God's understanding is infinite. Infinite in this verse is the Hebrew *micpar* and means the same thing as it does in English, that is, "having no boundaries or limits." Now, if God's understanding has no boundaries or limits, and understanding is predicated on knowledge, then it follows necessarily that God's knowledge has no boundaries or limitations. Such knowledge would be "unsearchable" by mere finite creatures, and this is exactly what the Bible says.[1] In other words, the Bible teaches that God "knows all things."[2] This kind of knowledge is what the theologians call "omniscience." By definition, omniscience or "all-knowingness" encompasses the present, the past, and the future, and undoubtedly includes genuine foreknowledge.[3] This is proved by many Bible passages. In the space that follows, we will notice a few of these.

Just before he died, Moses was told by God of the coming apostasy of the Israelites.[4] In doing so, God was not just declaring what He planned to do in the future, He was making it clear that He knew what human beings would be doing in the future of their own free wills. In Acts 2:23, the apostle Peter taught that Jesus was delivered up "by the determined purpose and foreknowledge of

---

1 See Romans 11:33.

2 1 John 3:20.

3 By genuine, I mean that God actually has the ability to foreknow the future, contingent, free will choices of men and women.

4 Deuteronomy 31:16-21.

God." He went on to say to the Jews, "...you have taken [Jesus] by lawless hands, have crucified [Him], and put [Him] to death." This clearly teaches that God's plan to deliver up His Son was made in view of what He foreknew the Jews and Romans would do, that is, He knew that given the right circumstances, they would cause Jesus to be crucified. Again, in Romans 8:28-30 and 1 Peter 1:1-2, we are told that God foreknew certain individuals, of their own free wills, would obey the gospel and be conformed to the image of His Son, that they would become the "elect" in their connection with Jesus Christ. This means that God's foreknowledge of those who would be conformed to the image of His Son predates their election and predestination. Since God chose them "in Christ" before the creation of the world,[5] it seems clear that they and their free will actions were foreknown by God before the world began. Therefore, there is absolutely no reason for the Bible believer to ever doubt God's genuine foreknowledge of the future, contingent, free will choices of His creatures.

Calvinists assert that God's foreknowledge and man's free will are completely irreconcilable. Again, they are wrong! The Bible teaches that God has foreknowledge (and we will look at some biblical examples of these momentarily), therefore, God's foreknowledge is a fact. Likewise, the Bible teaches that man has free will (and we have already examined some of these passages), therefore, man's free moral agency is a fact. Consequently, Calvinists, or anyone else, who claim that God's foreknowledge and man's free will are incompatible are teaching that which is contrary to God's word.

---

[5] Ephesians 1:4.

A Little Simple Logic

Notwithstanding, Calvinists and other determinists attempt to vindicate their position by arguing as follows:

> Necessarily, whatever God foreknows comes to pass
> and
> God foreknew that *x* would come to pass,
> therefore, it follows that
> Necessarily, *x* will come to pass.

And so, the determinists argue, if God foreknows the future, then all things come to pass necessarily, and this means that man's free moral agency and true contingency are eliminated, and were never more than a non-determinist's illusion. But, and this seems difficult for some, the above reasoning embraces a logical fallacy. According to the rules of logic, the conclusion of an argument can be necessary only if both of the premises are necessary. But in the above argument, only the major premise is a necessary truth. The minor premise is not a necessary truth because it is not necessary that God know *x*. He could have known *y* instead. Consequently, the proper conclusion to the above syllogism is:

> Therefore, *x* will come to pass.

Now, from the fact that God foreknows that *x* will occur, we may be sure that *x* will, in fact, occur; but, and this is my point, it is not *necessary* that *x* occur. It is, indeed, possible (because man is a free moral agent) that *x* might not occur. This having been said, we do know, according to the above syllogism, that *x* will actually occur because God foreknew it would occur.[6] The fact that God knows I will act a certain way does not mean His knowledge causes me to act this way. If, as a free moral agent, I chose to behave differently, God's knowledge about this behavior would also be different. In other words, if God foreknew that I should do *x*, then I will do x. But, as a free moral agent, I have the power not to do *x*, and if I were not to do *x*, then God would not have known that I will do *x*. This means that although God's foreknowledge is chronologically prior to my action, my action is logically prior to His foreknowledge. What this all means is that the future, contingent, free will choices of men and women are not settled by God's foreknowledge; instead, God's foreknowledge is settled by the reality of the future events themselves. The fact that God, from His viewpoint in eternity, sees them "ahead of time" does not mean these events will happen because God sees them; rather, they are going to happen because of the genuine free moral agency of those involved. Again, the fact that God sees them ahead of time does not make them happen in any causative sense.

I want you to notice that the Bible does not say that God has the capacity to know all things, which He certainly does; instead, the argument is that God actually "knows all things." Now, if God knows all things, what is it that He does not know? Remember, the Great Intelligence of the universe is writing to His intelligent creatures. Consequently, not only does He teach us through direct

---

[6] It is extremely unfortunate that when we begin to talk about logic some people's eyes begin to glaze over. Many seem convinced that logic is very difficult, but it is really not as hard as they think. Without the rules of logic, we could not understand anything. Without logic, God would be unable to communicate His will to us. Even if He were to directly inspire us, we would still need to follow the rules of logic in order to understand and apply His words.

statements and approved examples, but He also expects us to come to necessary conclusions about what He has written. By direct statement, the Bible teaches that God "knows all things."[7] By direct statement, the Bible teaches that God's understanding is without boundaries or limits.[8] Therefore, if God's understanding is infinite, and understanding is established through knowledge, then it follows necessarily that God's knowledge is also infinite. In other words, based on the direct statements of Scripture, the only conclusion one can arrive at is that there is nothing God does not know and this encompasses the then, the now, and the not yet!

Some Claim God Cannot Know The Future

Calvin's starting point was that God's foreknowledge and man's free will are mutually exclusive. Calvin opted for God's foreknowledge at the expense of man's free will. Others, while rejecting Calvin's false system, have believed his premise. Consequently, they have opted for man's free will at the expense of God's foreknowledge. Presently, there are New Testament Christians who are taking this position. Giving lip-service to the omniscience of God,[9] they claim that because the future does not yet exist, God cannot know what does not yet exist, unless He, by His decretive will, intends to bring these events to pass. They claim that passages that depict God as knowing the end from the beginning[10] are really examples of God's omnipotence, not His foreknowledge. God, they claim, simply cannot know the future,

[7] 1 John 3:20.
[8] See Psalm 147:5.
[9] They acknowledge that God knows the past and present perfectly.
[10] See Isaiah 46:10; Romans 4:17.

contingent, free will choices of men and women. These brethren are just as wrong as the Calvinists they condemn. All the Bible passages that show God foreknowing the future, contingent, free will choices of individuals and groups (and we have mentioned some of these earlier) testify to the error these brethren espouse.

On the other hand, there are brethren who believe that God has the capacity to know all things, but for reasons known only to Him, He chooses not to know some things. Unlike those who say God cannot know, this group does not take their position for philosophical reasons. Instead, they take their position because the Bible does seem to be saying there are things God does (did) not know,[11] and as they are wont to say, "We all know the Bible does not contradict itself." True, the Bible does not contradict itself. Therefore, if the Bible teaches that God knows all things, then passages like Genesis 18 and 22 must be interpreted in light of this truth. In fact, a fundamental rule of Bible interpretation says that we must understand Scripture in its normal sense unless a literal interpretation contradicts other clear teaching found in God's Word. Not doing this, in my opinion, is the error one makes in thinking these passages negate the all-knowingness of God.[12]

Mixing Apples And Oranges

In their defense, many who take the above position argue that just as God being all-powerful does not mean He has to be doing everything He has the capacity to do, being all-knowing does not mean that God must actually know everything He has the capacity

---

11 For example, Genesis 18:21 and 22:12.

12 If you disagree with me, I would be very interested to know what you think Psalm 147:5, Romans 11:33, and John 3:20 are saying about God's omniscience.

to know. What to many seems like iron-clad logic is, in fact, a *non sequitur*, that is, it is simply an argument that does not logically follow the premise or evidence. Therefore, comparing omniscience with omnipotence is like confusing apples and oranges. Yes, it is true that being all-powerful, definitionally, does not mean one has to be engaged in doing all things. On the other hand, by definition, knowing all things means knowing all things. Being all-powerful infers ability only, while being all-knowing infers not just ability but the actual knowledge itself, which, in the case of God, is universal in scope. In other words, God is not claiming that He could know all things; He's claiming He does know all things! Those who wrongly believe Genesis 18 and 22 to be teaching that God has chosen not to know some things are explaining away, by their literal interpretation of these passages, the plain teaching of those scriptures I have cited which clearly teach the all-knowingness of God. Evidently, they must think the passages I have cited mean something other than what they literally say. But, whether one agrees with me or not, the task before us is to harmonize two seemingly contradictory teachings—God knows all things; God does not know some things—and do it in a way that does no harm to the integrity of either set of scriptures.

Resolving An Apparent Dilemma

Here is how I resolve what otherwise appears to be a dilemma. In Genesis 18:21, we are dealing with an unusual circumstance. God, who is omnipresent, which means He is equally present to all of space simultaneously, has, on occasion, entered space at specific points and become present in it for a specific purpose. The theologians call these occurrences "theophanies." This seems to be the case in Genesis 18:21. In verse 1 of the chapter, it says, "Then the Lord appeared to him by the terebinth trees of Mamre, as he was sitting in the tent door in the heat of the day." In verse 2, it mentions "three men." Whether these three men are manifestations of the triune nature of God, or whether the other two were angels, is not clear. What seems clear is that this is, in fact, a theophany. In entering the time/space continuum, God, who is infinite in His being, willingly, and somehow, without ceasing to be who He is, allowed Himself to be subject to the finite. It's mind-boggling, I know. Nevertheless, this appears to be the clear import of Scripture. Let us now look at Genesis 18:21 with my interpretation interjected in brackets:

> *I, [who have somehow subjected Myself to the time/space continuum] will go down [not from heaven, but down the way geographically]* ***now*** *[not in eternity, but right now at this moment, subject to time and space] and see [i.e., learn experientially in time and space] whether they have done [and, more importantly, continue to do "****now****"] altogether according to the outcry against it that has come to Me [in eternity, not limited by time and space]; and if not [i.e., if they are no longer doing what I knew they were doing before I allowed Myself to be subject to time and space], I [God subject to time and space] will know [experientially].*

Notice that I have emphasized the word "now" by putting it in bold letters. This is because I believe this word to be the key to understanding this passage. God, who knows the past, present, and future, confines His knowing to the "now" of the time/space continuum. Are we supposed to think that the self-existent, eternal, infinite Spirit who is God did not really know everything that had been happening in Sodom and Gomorrah? 1 John 3:20 makes it absolutely clear that God is greater than our heart (He knows our heart as well as every other heart) and knows all things. Consequently, whatever Genesis 18:21 means must be understood by the context, and the context clearly indicates a theophany. And so, the theophany must be taken into consideration when trying to understand this passage. When I debated a brother who teaches that there are some things God cannot know, he at least admitted that God knew the past and present perfectly. Now, some are wanting me to believe that the all-knowing God does not even know the past and present perfectly. This, of course, is the only conclusion one may come to if Genesis 18:21 is to be understood literally and apart from the "now" context. Consequently, this conclusion is not, nor can it be, true.

I now call your attention to what I consider to be the more difficult passage. In Genesis 22:12, the angel of the Lord says to Abraham, "Do not lay your hand on the lad, or do anything to him; for now I know that you fear God, since you have not withheld your son, your only son, from Me." Although the "angel of the Lord," who some think may be the pre-incarnate Christ, is involved in this episode, the unusual circumstances associated with a theophany are not a part of the context. Even so, as has already been pointed out, the Bible teaches that the self-existent, eternal, and infinite Spirit who is God "knows all things." So, once again, citing a fundamental principle of Bible interpretation, the current passage cannot be interpreted in a way that would negate clear and unequivocal passages which teach that God knows all things.

As we think about this situation, it is interesting to note what the self-existent, eternal, infinite Spirit who is God knew about Abraham before He ever "tested" him. In Genesis 18:17-19, the Lord said:

> *Shall I hide from Abraham what I am doing, since Abraham shall surely become a great and mighty nation, and all the nations of the earth shall be blessed in him? For I have known him, in order that he may command his children and his household*

after him, that they keep the way of the Lord, to do righteousness and justice, that the Lord may bring to Abraham what He has spoken to him.

In other words, God knew that Abraham would pass the "tests" of faith, which included the one mentioned in this passage. To disregard this information, as well as the truth about God's "all-knowingness," is to make a serious mistake when trying to understand this passage.

Yes, taken literally, the passage does appear to be teaching that God learned something about Abraham that He had not previously known. But, if God really does know all things, and if He therefore knew Abraham would pass all "tests," then Genesis 22:12 cannot be teaching what it seems to be teaching.

I admit to feeling just a little bit uncomfortable making this kind of statement. Nevertheless, I am confident this is the correct way to view this passage. Paul was not the only inspired writer who wrote things difficult to understand, which, if we are not careful, can be twisted to teach something completely contrary to truth.[13] Our responsibility is to "Be diligent to present [ourselves] approved to God, [as workers] who [do not] need to be ashamed, rightly dividing the word of truth."[14]This is not always easy, but if we work hard at it, then we, too, will pass the "test."

I believe the key to understanding Genesis 22:12 is to be found in places like Deuteronomy 29-30, where God promises to give life or death and blessings or cursings, depending upon one's obedience to His Word. Do what is right and one is blessed; do what is wrong and one is cursed. This is a principle taught many places in the Bible, and although we do not expect to hear the voice of the

[13] See 2 Peter 3:16.

[14] 2 Timothy 2:15.

"angel of the Lord" today, nevertheless, if we serve the Lord faithfully, He will bless us; if we disobey Him, He will curse us.

God is all-knowing. However, He has graciously agreed to deal with us in the time/space continuum. In Genesis 22:12, I have once again emphasized the word "now." This is because I believe the key to understanding this passage, like the key to understanding Genesis 18:21, is the "now" context. In the now of Abraham's time and space, the voice of the angel of the Lord could be heard audibly, and God is acknowledging His blessing on or appreciation of Abraham at a very critical time and place in his "walk of faith." In fact, the word "know" in this passage is sometimes translated "to recognize, admit, acknowledge, confess, declare, or tell." So, in harmony with the rest of Scripture, and without doing any violence to the words of this passage, Genesis 22:12 is not teaching that the all-knowing God of the universe did not really know whether Abraham would pass this critical test. He is, instead, acknowledging His appreciation of Abraham's faithfulness to Him. In other words, He is declaring, "Abraham, I have been testing you...and you have passed the test!"

As has been demonstrated, there is nothing in God's word that limits His knowledge, not even the free moral agency of man. Therefore, with the apostle Paul, we say: "Now to the King eternal, immortal, invisible, to God who alone is wise, be honor and glory forever and ever. Amen."[15]

---

[15] 1 Timothy 1:17.

Chapter 5

The Five Points Of Calvinism Stated And Examined

There are five main pillars upon which the superstructure of Calvinism rests. These are technically known as "The Five Points of Calvinism."[1] In this section, we will make a critical examination of each of these, holding them up to the light of Scripture. It should be understood that the Five Points are not random, isolated, nor independent doctrines. Rather, they are "so inter-related that they form a simple, harmonious, self-consistent system."[2] Calvinism, although terribly flawed, is amazingly logical in its parts. If one were to concede that the first point of Calvinism (viz., "Total Depravity") were true, then all four of the following points would necessarily follow. Of course, the opposite is also true. Prove any one of the Five Points of Calvinism wrong and the entire system must be surrendered.

Total Depravity

In the Westminster Confession, the doctrine of Total Depravity is stated as follows: "Man, by his fall into a state of sin, hath

---

1 The Five Points can be readily remembered if they are associated with the acrostic T-U-L-I-P, which stands for: **T**, Total Depravity; **U**, Unconditional Election; **L**, Limited Atonement; **I**, Irresistible Grace; and **P**, Perseverance of the Saints.

2 Boettner, *op. cit.*, page 59.

wholly lost all ability of will to any spiritual good accompanying salvation; so as a natural man, being altogether averse from good, and dead in sin, is not able, by his own strength, to convert himself, or to prepare himself thereunto."[3] For obvious reasons, many Calvinists call this the doctrine of "Total Inability" or, as we will see in a moment, the doctrine of "Original Sin." In his book, *The Bondage of the Will*, which argues that man's will is bound as a result of the fall of man and its effect, Martin Luther said that man is born with a "total inability to will good."[4] According to this position, all mankind is totally depraved. The essence of this false doctrine is the total inability of man to do anything truly good in God's sight, especially the inability to do anything toward receiving salvation. Again, this total depravity is not acquired, as non-determinists teach, but innate. Therefore, "to become sinful, men do not wait until the age of accountable actions arrive. Rather, they are apostates from the womb."[5]

Although the doctrine of Total Depravity is crucial to all forms of determinism, whether Augustinian, Lutheran, or Calvinistic, it is not really as important to the general system of Calvinism as it is to the Five Points. As we observed previously, if the doctrine of Total Depravity is defeated, all of the other Points are defeated. Nevertheless, the more important concept to Calvinism is the Sovereign's "Eternal Decree." In other words, contrary to what Calvinists want us to believe, Calvinism does not have as its "starting point the fact that all mankind sinned in Adam."[6] Calvinism starts with what they call the Eternal Decree, which the *Westminster*

---

[3] Chapter IX, Section III.

[4] Page 199.

[5] Boettner, page 66.

[6] *Ibid.*, page 61.

Confession explains thus: "God from all eternity did by the most wise and holy counsel of His own will, freely and unchangeably ordain whatsoever comes to pass."[7] In other words, the essence of Calvinism is its doctrine of Predestination. About this, Calvin said: "Predestination we call the eternal decree of God, by which He has determined in Himself, what He would have to become of every individual of mankind. For they are not all created with a similar destiny; but eternal life is foreordained for some and eternal death for others. Every man, therefore, being created for one or the other of these ends, we say is predestined either to life or to death."[8] Therefore, the supposed bondage of man's will is the direct result of an alleged Eternal Decree, and only secondarily the result of an argument for Total Depravity. This point was made earlier in the sections on sovereignty and free will, and I do not intend to rehash it here. I mention it only because the problem of Total Depravity causes some real sticky problems for determinists, particularly when the salvation/damnation of infants is raised. The Augustinians handle it one way, and the Calvinists handle it another. The way the Calvinists deal with the problem proves that Calvinism does not begin with the doctrine of Original Sin.

The Thorny Issue Of Infant Salvation

In formulating the doctrine of Original Sin, Augustine taught that, since the fall, all men are born totally depraved. According to him, a child who died before reaching the age of accountability was lost because of the "sinful nature" he inherited from Adam. Believing, as he did, in the idea of baptismal regeneration, Augustine

---

7 Quoted in Boettner, page 13.

8 *Institutes of the Christian Religion*, Book III, Chapter XXI, Section 5.

believed only a "baptized" infant could be saved. He said, "As nothing else is done for children in baptism but their being incorporated into the church, that is, connected with the body and members of Christ, it follows that when this is not done for them they belong to perdition."[9] Thus, the practice of infant baptism was begun. Roman Catholicism, which proudly claims Augustine as its own, has been instrumental in keeping this erroneous doctrine alive down through the centuries. Of course, the idea of infants being eternally lost in hell was so repugnant to most people that it was eventually "determined" by the Roman Catholic Church that unbaptized infants did not really go to hell at all. Instead, they went to a special place called "Limbo," which was not heaven, but it certainly was not hell either. In this way, when it came to the subject of dear, precious infants dying and going to hell, the shocking and horrifying consequence of Total Depravity was lightened somewhat by the doctrine of Limbo, which was never more than the figment of some Catholic cleric's imagination.

On the other hand, Calvinists "solved" this problem by appealing to the doctrine of Predestination. Yes, they said, infants inherit Adam's sin all right, but if God has predestined or eternally decreed that an infant would be saved, and this apart from anything the infant would or would not do, then the infant would be saved by the same unmerited grace that saves an adult. Remember, unlike all determinists, Calvinists believe that all men, apart from anything they will or will not do, are predestined or foreordained to be eternally saved or eternally lost. Speaking to this, Dr. Benjamin B. Warfield said: "Their destiny is determined irrespective of their choice, by an unconditional decree of God, suspended

[9] *On the Merits and Forgiveness of Sins*, A.D. 417.

for its execution on no act of their own; and their salvation is wrought by an unconditional application of the grace of Christ to their souls, through the immediate and irresistible operation of the Holy Spirit prior to and apart from any action of their own proper wills...This is but to say that they are unconditionally predestinated to salvation from the foundation of the world."[10]

The *Westminster Confession* says, "Elect infants, dying in infancy, are regenerated and saved by Christ."[11] This left the impression with some that there are non-elect infants, who, dying in infancy, are lost, and that the Presbyterian Church teaches this as their doctrine. In denying this, some have said: "The history of the phrase 'Elect infants dying in infancy' makes clear that the contrast implied was not between 'elect infants dying in infancy' and 'non-elect infants dying in infancy,' but rather between 'elect infants dying in infancy' and 'elect infants living to grow up.'"[12] In order to correct any misunderstanding, in 1903, the Presbyterian Church in the U. S. A. adopted a Declaratory Statement which reads as follows: "With reference to Chapter X, Section 3, of the Confession of Faith, that it is not to be regarded as teaching that any who die in infancy are lost. We believe that all dying in infancy are included in the election of grace, and are regenerated and saved by Christ through the Spirit, who works when and where and how He pleases." Calvin's view of this is explained by Dr. R. A. Webb in the following paragraph:

> *Calvin teaches that all the reprobate 'procure'—that is his own word—their own personal and conscious acts of 'impiety,' 'wickedness,' and 'rebellion.' Now reprobate infants, though*

---

10 *Two Studies in the History of Doctrine*, page 230.

11 Chapter X, Section 3.

12 Dr. S. G. Craig, *Christianity Today*, January 1931, page 14.

> *guilty of original sin and under condemnation, cannot, while they are infants, thus 'procure' their own destruction by their personal acts of impiety, wickedness, and rebellion. They must, therefore, live to the years of moral responsibility in order to perpetrate the acts of impurity, wickedness, and rebellion, which Calvin defines as the mode through which they procure their destruction...Consequently, [Calvin's] own reasoning compels him to hold (to be consistent with himself), that no reprobate child can die in infancy; but all must live to the age of moral accountability, and translate original sin into actual sin.*[13]

So, there you have it, any child who dies in infancy is saved! With this, Calvinists avoid the heart-rending idea of little babies dying in sin and going to hell. Therefore, Total Depravity is really not the starting point for Calvinism. However, it is now time to turn our attention to a critical examination of the doctrine of Total Depravity.

The Doctrine Stated And Refuted

The doctrine stated: Calvin, as had Augustine and Luther before him, argued that all mankind sinned in Adam. In one of their catechisms it is stated like this: "All mankind...sinned in him [Adam], and fell with him in that first transgression... The sinfulness of that estate whereinto man fell, consisteth in the guilt of Adam's first sin."[14]

The doctrine refuted: But, the Bible teaches that everyone bears the guilt of his own sins, not the sin of Adam: "The soul who sins shall die. The son shall not bear the guilt of the father, nor the father bear the guilt of the son. The righteousness of the righteous shall be upon himself, and the wickedness of the wicked shall be

---

13 *Calvin Memorial Address*, page 112.

14 *The Larger Catechism*, Questions 22, 25.

upon himself."[15] The Bible makes it clear that one obeys the gospel in order to have his own sins blotted out, not the sin of Adam: "Repent therefore and be converted, that your sins may be blotted out."[16] Furthermore, when we all "appear before the judgment seat of Christ," we will give an answer for what we have done in the flesh, not what Adam did.[17] Finally, it is our own sins, not Adam's, which separate us from God.[18]

The doctrine stated: "Fallen man...lacks the power of spiritual discernment. His reason or understanding is blinded, and the taste and feelings are perverted."[19] Denying that man has free will, and affirming that he cannot, without having been predestined by God, choose to do good or evil, Loraine Boettner went on to say: "Hence we deny the existence in man of a power which may act either way, on the logical ground that both virtue and vice cannot come out of a moral condition of the agent... He is incapable of understanding, and much less of doing, the things of God."[20] The argument is that unregenerate man is "dead in sin," and like anyone who is physically dead is unable to perform anything physical, the spiritually dead man is completely unable to perform anything spiritual.

The doctrine refuted: Yes, the Bible teaches that before we are regenerated, born again, raised, or made alive, we are "dead in trespasses and sins."[21] But the Bible just as clearly teaches that the unregenerate man can indeed "obey from the heart" the form of

---

15 Ezekiel 18:20.

16 Acts 3:19.

17 2 Corinthians 5:10.

18 See Isaiah 59:1, 2.

19 Boettner, page 64.

20 *Ibid.*, pages 65, 67.

21 Ephesians 2:1.

doctrine that he has been taught, that is, the gospel.[22] In Colossians 2:12-13, the apostle Paul said it this way: "Buried with Him in baptism, in which you also were raised with Him through faith in the working of God, who raised Him from the dead. And you, being dead in your trespasses and the uncircumcision of your flesh, He has made alive together with Him, having forgiven you all trespasses." Faith, of course, comes by hearing the gospel.[23] Then having heard the gospel, one must believe it,[24] repent of his sins,[25] and confess with his mouth that he believes Jesus is Christ.[26] But in doing all this, one has done that which the Calvinists teach an unregenerate man cannot do. That baptism is clearly under discussion in Colossians 2:12-13 cannot be denied. That this passage teaches that one is not "raised" (verse 12) or "made alive" (verse 13) until he has submitted to baptism also cannot be denied. That the expressions "raised" and "made alive" refer to being regenerated should be just as clear. In fact, there seems little doubt that the "washing of regeneration" mentioned in Titus 3:5 is referring to baptism. The fact that one could be doing something "through faith," as Colossians 2:12 clearly teaches, before being regenerated flies in the face of Calvinist claims. This, no doubt, is why Calvinists deny that water baptism has anything to do with being regenerated or born again.

The doctrine stated: Speaking of the "depth of man's corruption," Boettner argues: "It is wholly beyond [man's] own power to cleanse himself. His only hope of an amendment of life lies accordingly in a change of heart, which change is brought about by the

---

22 See Romans 6:17.

23 Romans 10:17.

24 Mark 16:16.

25 Acts 17:30.

26 Acts 8:37; Romans 10:10.

sovereign re-creative power of the Holy Spirit who works when and where and how He pleases."[27] Without this direct operation of the Holy Spirit, man "cannot be convinced of the truth of the Gospel by any amount of external testimony."[28]

The doctrine refuted: The "gift" or "renewing" of the Holy Spirit comes after water baptism,[29] which, again, goes against the theological grain of Calvinism. Furthermore, the Bible says the Holy Spirit is given to all those who "obey" the Lord,[30] something the Calvinists say cannot occur without a direct operation of the Holy Spirit. Therefore, it should be clear that what Calvinists teach about Total Depravity is totally false.

Unconditional Election

If the doctrine of Total Depravity be admitted, the doctrine of Unconditional Election necessarily follows. Of course, we no more admit the doctrine of Unconditional Election than we do that of Total Depravity. In fact, by their own admission, which says that if the doctrine of Total Depravity be disproved, all the other Five Points crumble, we have already proven Calvinism to be a reprobate system. Nevertheless, we now proceed to demonstrate the total inconsistency of any and all parts of Calvinism with the truths taught in God's word.

The Doctrine Stated And Refuted

The doctrine stated: If man is born totally depraved and does not have free will, which is what Calvinists clearly teach, then he does

---

27 *Op. cit.*, page 68.
28 *Ibid.*
29 Acts 2:38; Titus 3:5.
30 Acts 5:32.

not have the ability to do those things God has commanded him to do. Therefore, if a man is going to be saved, God, totally independent of any foreknown choices man will make, chooses (elects) him to salvation. This means, "A man is not saved because he believes in Christ; he believes in Christ because he is saved."[31] In other words, "The elect of God are chosen by Him to be His children, in order that they might be made to believe, not because He foresaw that they would believe."[32] Incidentally, this also was the view espoused by Augustine and Luther. Accordingly: "Foreordination in general cannot rest on foreknowledge; for only that which is certain can be foreknown, and only that which is predetermined can be certain... God foreknows only because He has pre-determined. His foreknowledge is but a transcript of His will as for what shall come to pass in the future... His foreknowledge of what is yet to be, whether it be in regard to the world as a whole or in regard to the detailed life of every individual, rests upon His pre-arranged plan."[33]

The doctrine refuted: First of all, the doctrine of Unconditional Election was defeated when Total Depravity was demonstrated to be false. Second, it is clear that Calvinists do not believe God actually has foreknowledge (viz., prescience). According to them, God "foreknows" what is going to happen because He has determined it will happen. We would be fools to deny the reality of this statement. This kind of statement is what the logicians call a tautology, that is, a needless repetition that cannot be anything other than logically true. For example, to say that God has predestined whatever is going to happen, therefore, He foreknows whatever is

---

31 Boettner, page 101.

32 *Ibid.*

33 Boettner, page 99.

going to happen is similar to saying, "God knows He is going to do something, therefore, He knows He is going to do something." Such would be needless and foolish repetition. Nevertheless, this is how Calvinists interpret all references to God's foreknowledge.

Although it is true that there are passages that declare God can speak of future events as definite because of His decretive will,[34] this is not the way foreknowledge is usually used in the Scriptures. Furthermore, it is ironic that one of the favorite passages of the Calvinists states unequivocally that God's predestination of certain future events was dependent upon His foreknowledge, and not the other way around, as they claim. In Romans 8:29, 30, the apostle Paul says: "For whom He foreknew, He also predestined to be conformed to the image of His Son, that He might be the firstborn among many brethren. Moreover whom He predestined, these He also called; whom He called, these He also justified; and whom He justified, these He also glorified." Now, there may be legitimate disagreement with reference to all the ramifications of this passage, but there seems to be no legitimate reason to reject the idea conveyed here that God's predestination was dependent upon actual foreknowledge. It is not insignificant that the apostle Peter, under the same inspiration that guided the apostle Paul, makes precisely the same point when he mentioned those who were "elect according to the foreknowledge of God the Father, in sanctification of the Spirit, for obedience and sprinkling of the blood of Jesus Christ."[35] We can find no hint in the Scriptures, or among the so-called "Church Fathers" before Augustine, that foreknowledge (Greek *proginsko*) was used in any way other than to mean "knowledge in advance." In other words, the Bible teaches that God's

---

34 See Isaiah 46:10.

35 1 Peter 1:2.

"knowing in advance" allowed Him to choose, predestinate or elect those who would be saved in connection with His Son Jesus, that is, those who would, of their own free wills, be "conformed to the image of His Son."[36]

God indeed has foreknowledge, even of the future, contingent, free will choices of men and women. This allows Him to choose, foreordain, predestine, or elect individuals without violating their free wills. This view of foreknowledge agrees perfectly with Acts 2:23, which says, "Him [Jesus Christ], being delivered by the determined purpose and foreknowledge of God [the Father], you have taken by lawless hands, have crucified, and put to death." This means that the Father designed His plan to deliver up His Son with a view as to what the Jews and Romans would do—that is, if given the opportunity, they would crucify Him. If this is not what this passage is teaching, then it is reduced to a needless tautology that says, "God determined to offer up His Son, therefore, He knew He would offer up His Son."

The doctrine stated: Calvinists teach that God's plan not only deals with mankind *in toto*, but that He also has a plan for particular individuals whom He unconditionally elects to salvation and eternal life. As proof, they cite passages like 2 Thessalonians 2:13, which says, "But we are bound to give thanks to God always for you, brethren beloved by the Lord, because God from the beginning chose you for salvation through sanctification by the Spirit and belief in the truth," and Acts 13:48, which says: "Now when the Gentiles heard this, they were glad and glorified the word of the Lord. And as many as had been appointed to eternal life believed."

---

[36] Romans 8:29.

The doctrine refuted: Calvinists teach the unconditional election of particular individuals to eternal salvation. As a result, some have thought that in rejecting Calvinism they must deny the election of particular individuals. I believe this to be a serious mistake in that it makes Calvinism more difficult to refute and, even more important, it appears to be a denial of what the Scriptures teach on this subject. The problem with Unconditional Election is not that it deals with particular individuals, but that it alleges these individuals are elected unconditionally. This last point the Bible clearly denies. Individuals are elected, predestinated, or foreordained, and these are all scriptural terms, to eternal salvation based upon God's foreknowledge of their free will choices to "obey the gospel," thus being "conformed to the image of His Son."[37] This does not, as Calvinists claim, make man's will sovereign. It was God, of His own free will, who decided to extend His plan of salvation to man. Therefore, even though His foreknowledge informed Him there would be those who would be conformed to the image of His Son and, therefore, be saved, it was entirely up to Him whether He tendered the plan. Without God's plan, man could have done nothing to effect his own salvation. Therefore, in one sense, we are saved by God's grace and not our works. This is precisely what Paul was talking about in Ephesians 2:4-10, where he says:

> *But God, who is rich in mercy, because of His great love with which He loved us, even when we were dead in trespasses, made us alive together with Christ (by grace you have been saved), and raised us up together, and made us sit together in the heavenly places in Christ Jesus, that in the ages to come He might show the exceeding riches of His grace in His kindness toward us in Christ*

[37] See Romans 8:29, 30; 1 Peter 1:2.

> *Jesus. For by grace you have been saved through faith, and that not of yourselves; it is the gift of God, not of works, lest anyone should boast. For we are His workmanship, created in Christ Jesus for good works, which God prepared beforehand that we should walk in them.*

Salvation, then, is an undeserved, unmerited gift from God, for this is the meaning of the word "grace."

But in another sense, and this because man has free will, salvation is something man must work out for himself. About this, the apostle Paul said, "Therefore, my beloved, as you have always obeyed, not as in my presence only, but now much more in my absence, work out your own salvation with fear and trembling."[38] Elsewhere, the apostle Peter said, "Save yourselves from this crooked generation."[39] In these passages, the Bible teaches that a man, of his own free will, must, in order to be saved, respond, and continue to respond, to the demands of God's preceptive will. As such, faith and works work together to produce salvation.[40] Man working out his own salvation and thereby saving himself does not mean, as Calvinists erroneously think, that God is forced to give up His sovereignty. God forbid! In the verse immediately following the command for Christians to work out their own salvation, Paul said, "for it is God who works in you both to will and to do for His good pleasure."[41] In other words, just because God grants man free will does not mean He has relinquished control of the scheme of redemption. This is further illustrated by Paul's prayer for the Christians at Ephesus, in which he asked God to grant

---

38 Philippians 2:12.
39 Acts 2:40, ASV.
40 See James 2:14-26.
41 Philippians 2:13.

them, "according to the riches of His glory, to be strengthened with might through His Spirit in the inner man."[42] The "gift" of the Holy Spirit to obedient believers[43] functions as God's "guarantee" that He is still in control of man's redemption[44] which, in turn, causes us to be confident that He is able to finish the work He has started in us right up to the day of Jesus Christ.[45] Consequently, "we know that all things work together for good to those who love God, to those who are the called according to His purpose."[46]

The Scheme of Redemption was "predestined according to the purpose of Him who works all things according to the counsel of His will."[47] Therefore, it was not a plan that would or could fail. Even so, the plan would be no small undertaking. It would ultimately take the sacrifice of the heavenly Father's only begotten Son,[48] the divine Logos,[49] who would sooner or later have to leave heaven, take upon Himself the mantle of flesh,[50] and finally shed His blood on the cruel cross of Calvary for the remission of our sins.[51] As such, this was not simply *a* plan, it was, instead, *the* plan! It was the plan that would work because God's foreknowledge would allow Him to not just design a plan that could, under certain circumstances, work, but it would also allow Him to carry out this

---

[42] Ephesians 3:16.
[43] See Acts 2:38; 5:32.
[44] 2 Corinthians 5:5.
[45] Philippians 1:6.
[46] Romans 8:28.
[47] Ephesians 1:11.
[48] John 3:16-18.
[49] John 1:1.
[50] John 1:14.
[51] Matthew 26:28.

plan with absolutely impeccable precision.[52] As the result of this perfect plan, God would be able to "bring many sons unto glory."[53] These "many sons" were foreknown by the Father,[54] and this allowed him to design and put in motion a plan that would ultimately end in their glorification with Jesus in heaven.[55] Hence, in the mind of God, and this is a mind that knows the future, contingent, free will choices of men and women, the Scheme of Redemption is a "done deal."

According to Strong's Greek and Hebrew Lexicon, the Greek word *proorizo*, translated in the KJV as "predestinate," means to "predetermine," "decide beforehand," or "foreordain." As already noted, this does not mean that God in eternity made a choice of those He would save independent of anything they would do of their own free wills. Rather, God ordained or decreed in eternity (i.e., He predestined) that those who were going to be saved would have to be "conformed to the image of His Son."[56] This means that God did not choose individuals to be saved unconditionally, as Calvinists teach. On the contrary, based upon His foreknowledge of the future, contingent, free will choices of His creatures, God predestined (i.e., determined beforehand) those who would be saved conditionally.[57] This is what the apostle Paul was referring to when he wrote: "...just as He [the Father] chose us in Him [Jesus Christ] before the foundation of the world, that we should be holy and without blame before Him in love, having predestined us to

---

52 Consider what is actually taught in Acts 2:23.

53 Hebrews 2:9, 10.

54 Romans 8:29.

55 Romans 8:30.

56 Romans 8:29.

57 The condition would be their free will conformity to the image of God's Son.

adoption as sons by Jesus Christ to Himself, according to the good pleasure of His will."[58]

In the context of 2 Timothy 2:19, the apostle Paul says that although the faith of some had been overthrown by false teachers, "Nevertheless the solid foundation of God stands, having this seal: 'The Lord knows those who are His,' and, 'Let everyone who names the name of Christ depart from iniquity.'" This is not just true now, but we are assured that even in eternity the Lord knew those who were His.[59] Further, He knows now, just as He did in eternity, who will eventually be glorified in heaven.[60] Is God sovereign? Yes. Is the Scheme of Redemption His plan? Yes. Is He continuing to work this plan? Yes. Does man have free will? Yes. Does God know the future, contingent, free will choices of men and women? Yes. The plan and its result (i.e., the bringing of many sons to glory) is certain not because God has predestined these many sons to salvation "without any foresight of faith or good works, or perseverance ...or any other thing in the creature, as conditions, or causes moving Him thereunto,"[61] but by God's "determined counsel and foreknowledge."[62] Even so, as free will creatures, we must be "even more diligent to make [our] call and election sure, for if [we] do these things [we] will never stumble."[63] Once again, Calvinism has shown itself to be seriously flawed theology.

---

58 Ephesians 1:4-5.

59 Ephesians 1:4.

60 Romans 8:30.

61 *Westminster Confession*, Chapter III, Section 3.

62 See Acts 2:23.

63 2 Peter 1:10.

Limited Atonement

Did Jesus offer Himself as a sacrifice for the whole human race, or did He die only for the elect? Calvinists teach that the Lord died for the elect only. This doctrine necessarily trails Unconditional Election. Therefore, it is already demonstrated to be false. Nevertheless, we will now proceed to examine the doctrine from a biblical perspective.

The Doctrine Stated And Refuted

The doctrine stated: *The Westminster Confession* says: "...Wherefore they who are elected being fallen in Adam, are redeemed in Christ, are effectually called unto faith in Christ by His Spirit working in due season; are justified, adopted, sanctified, and kept by His power through faith unto salvation. Neither are any other redeemed by Christ, effectually called, justified, adopted sanctified, and saved, but the elect only."[64] About this, Boettner says, "If from eternity God has planned to save one portion of the human race and not another, it seems to be a contradiction to say that His work has equal reference to both portions, or that He sent His Son to die for those whom He had predetermined not to save, as truly as, and in the same sense that He was sent to die for those whom He had chosen for salvation."[65]

The doctrine refuted: "For God so loved the world that He gave His only begotten Son, that whoever believes in Him should not perish but have everlasting life."[66] Again, "For the love of Christ compels us, because we judge thus: that if One died for all, then all died; and *He died for all*, that those who live should live no longer

[64] Chapter III, Section 6.

[65] Boettner, page 151.

[66] John 3:16.

for themselves, but for Him who died for them and rose again" (emphasis mine, AT).[67] Now, as if these two passages were not enough to refute the idea of a Limited Atonement, the Bible teaches unequivocally that it is God's will that all men come to the knowledge of the truth and be saved.[68] In 2 Peter 3:9, He is described as being "longsuffering toward us, not willing that any should perish but that all should come to repentance." These passages ought to be sufficient to demonstrate the error of Calvinism.

Irresistible Grace

If man is totally depraved and in this condition unable to do what is right, if he is unconditionally elected by God to salvation, and if Christ died only for the elect, then man, if he is to be saved, must be saved by Irresistible Grace. This is the logical progression exhibited in Calvinism. The problem with Calvinism is that it starts in the wrong place (viz., the Eternal Decree) and then proceeds to logically end up in all the wrong places (i.e., the Five Points of Calvinism). In the space that follows, we will examine and then refute the already disproved doctrine of Irresistible Grace.

The Doctrine Stated And Refuted

The doctrine stated: In pontificating this doctrine, the *Westminster Confession* says, "This effectual call [to salvation] is of God's free and special grace alone, not from any thing at all foreseen in man, who is altogether passive therein, until, being quickened and renewed by the Holy Spirit, he is thereby enabled to answer this

---

[67] 2 Corinthians 5:14, 15.

[68] 1 Timothy 2:4.

call, and to embrace the grace offered and conveyed by it."[69] In his book, *The Sovereignty of Grace*, Arthur C. Custance elaborates: "The only defense against Synergism [i.e., the idea that man works with God to some degree in coming to salvation] is an unqualified Calvinism ascribing all the glory to God by insisting upon the total spiritual impotence of man, an election based solely upon the good pleasure of God, an Atonement intended only for the elect though sufficient for all men, a grace that can neither be resisted nor earned, and a security for the believer that is as permanent as God Himself."[70] Therefore, it is clear Calvinists believe that God's saving grace cannot be resisted and is, therefore, irresistible. It is clear they believe that if grace can be resisted, then this "places God in the unworthy position of being dependent upon His creatures."[71] If grace can be resisted, then Calvinists believe this would mean God is no longer Sovereign.

The doctrine refuted: "The Lord is not slack concerning His promise, as some count slackness, but is longsuffering toward us, *not willing that any should perish* but that all should come to repentance" (italics mine, AT).[72] "Then Peter opened his mouth and said: In truth I perceive that God *shows no partiality*. But in every nation whoever fears Him and works righteousness is accepted by Him'" (italics mine, AT).[73] Would the God identified in these scriptures choose some to be saved apart from anything they would do of their own free wills, and then irresistibly bestow (force) His grace upon them so that they will be saved even when they might not want to be? Not hardly! Furthermore, the

69 Chapter X, Section 1 and 2.

70 Page 364.

71 Lewis S. Chafer, *Systematic Theology*, 1:230.

72 2 Peter 3:9.

73 Acts 10:34, 35.

necessary inference of 1 Thessalonians 5:19 is that the Spirit of God can be quenched. This cannot mean that the Holy Spirit Himself can be extinguished. Rather, it means that the influence the Holy Spirit exerts and urges upon us can be suppressed or stifled. Therefore, contrary to Calvinist doctrine, the Bible teaches that the God who wills (wants or desires) that all men come to the knowledge of the truth and be saved,[74] sends His Spirit into the world to convict men of their sins,[75] but that they can still, of their own free wills, reject His plan for them.[76] In other words, the Bible teaches the Holy Spirit can be resisted: "You stiff-necked and uncircumcised in heart and ears! You always resist the Holy Spirit; as your fathers did, so do you."[77]

As far as anyone knows, the first theologian to teach that God's will is always done and is never impeded by the will of any creature was Augustine (A.D. 354-430). Much later, the Reformers (viz., Luther, Calvin *et al.*) continued to tinker with Augustine's idea, rejecting some things here, modifying other things there, but generally refining it into a grand theological scheme. Calvin, of course, was the popular systematizer of that which now wears his name. Today, millions upon millions of religious people are held captive by the dogma of this false system. Even New Testament Christians have not been immune. Over the years, many have gotten caught up in the tentacles of Calvin's insidious system. Others, rightfully rejecting the Calvinism, have, nevertheless, espoused equally false ideas in their efforts to counter it. The Christian must always be very careful.[78] Those of us who think we are standing on the truth

---

[74] 1 Timothy 2:4.
[75] John 16:8.
[76] Luke 7:30.
[77] Acts 7:51.
[78] Ephesians 5:15.

of God's word must be careful "lest we fall" also.[79] This warning is never more important than when we are standing against the "wiles of the devil." If we fail to put on the "whole armor of God," we can be destroyed.[80] We must always fortify our defenses with book, chapter, and verse.[81]

Calvinists argue that in order for God to be Sovereign, He cannot be limited in what He would do by the pitiably insignificant wills of His finite creatures. In a sense, God is limited. The Bible says God "cannot lie."[82] In other words, "it is impossible for God to lie."[83] Nevertheless, this in no way affects His sovereignty. Even Calvinists would have to agree with this. Why? Because, they know that God's sovereignty, power, might, rule, etc. is not affected by self-limitations. God cannot lie because it is inconsistent with His nature, a nature that includes holiness, justice, righteousness, to name but a few. Therefore, things that are impossible with God because of who He is, do not mitigate either His Almightiness or Sovereignty. As we stated in the section on the Sovereignty of God, the key to Sovereignty is not causation, as the Calvinists believe, but control. God's permissive will allows Him the right to intervene in the decision-making process if His purposes demand it. Although He does not do this very often, allowing man, in most cases, to go his own way, nevertheless, He can and does intervene if necessary. This prerogative allows Him to exercise ultimate control over the life of every man and woman. By deciding of His own free will to make a creature who would himself possess free will, God agreed to limit Himself. This self-limitation does not destroy

[79] 1 Corinthians 10:12.
[80] See Ephesians 6:10-18.
[81] 1 Peter 4:11.
[82] Titus 1:2.
[83] Hebrews 6:18.

nor degrade His Sovereignty, regardless of what Calvinists think. Even so, it is just here that we must be very careful. The concept of self-limitation does not apply to the being of God, but only His actions. When it comes to who, what, and that God is, God cannot be anything other than who He is; that is, when God said to Moses, "I Am Who I Am,"[84] He was saying He was, is, and always will be who He is! Jesus, in addition to being a man, was also the "I Am."[85] Therefore, in taking upon Himself flesh, He did not quit being who He is! It was only in this sense that it could be said about Him that He "is the same yesterday, today, and forever."[86] Therefore, by His own definition of who, what, and that He is, God, as Deity, can never be anything other than who, what, and that He is. Therefore, He cannot limit or change His being, nor can He limit Himself by refusing to do something His nature requires. For example, God, although He is all-powerful, could not have saved man any number of ways. If He simply overlooked sin and forgave man, He would not be just, for justice demands that every sin receive a just recompense.[87] Therefore, in order for God to extend His mercy to man without violating His own just nature, He sent His Son to pay the price for our sins on the cruel cross of Calvary.[88] Without Christ paying the full price of our sins, reaping what He had not sown, God could not have saved us, for in doing so, He would have violated His own nature, which, when it comes to God, is impossible.

God can only limit Himself by choosing not to do those things which are not required by His nature. And since His nature does

[84] Exodus 3:14.

[85] John 8:58.

[86] Hebrews 13:8.

[87] Hebrews 2:2; Galatians 6:7, 8.

[88] Consider Romans 3:21-26, particularly verse 26.

not require Him to be the direct cause of everything, whether natural events or human actions, He is free to limit Himself with respect to these. Without this ability, you and I would not exist as we do, and even if we did, we could not be saved from our own sinfulness. Thank God we serve a Sovereign Ruler who can and has limited Himself.

The Perseverance Of The Saints

Like the others, this point does not stand alone, but follows logically the other four points of Calvinism.

The Doctrine Stated And Refuted

The doctrine stated: "They whom God hath accepted in His Beloved, effectually called and sanctified by His Spirit, can neither totally nor finally fall away from the state of grace; but shall certainly persevere therein to the end, and be eternally saved."[89] As Boettner says, "If God has chosen men absolutely and unconditionally to eternal life, and if the Spirit effectively applies to them the benefits of redemption, the inescapable conclusion is that these persons shall be saved."[90] He elaborates further: "Though floods of error deluge the land, though Satan raise all the powers of earth and all the iniquities of their own hearts against them, they shall never fail; but, persevering to the end, they shall inherit those mansions which have been prepared for them from the foundation of the world. The saints in heaven are happier but no more secure than are true believers here in this world."[91]

---

89 *Westminster Confession*, Chapter XVII, Section 1.
90 Boettner, page 182.
91 *Op. cit.*, pages 182, 183.

The doctrine refuted: Becoming a Christian is the most important decision one can make. When we obeyed the gospel, Jesus Christ became the absolute Lord of our lives. As a result, our past sins were graciously washed away by our Lord's precious blood, and we have been spiritually born again. There is, therefore, a crown of "glory" or "righteousness" now awaiting us in heaven.[92] Nothing nor no one can take away from us the salvation we now possess in connection with Christ Jesus. The apostle Paul, in Romans 8:35-39, drives this point home:

> *Who shall separate us from the love of Christ? Shall tribulation, or distress, or persecution, or famine, or nakedness, or peril, or sword? As it is written: 'For Your sake we are killed all day long; We are accounted as sheep for the slaughter.' Yet in all these things we are more than conquerors through Him who loved us. For I am persuaded that neither death nor life, nor angels nor principalities nor powers, nor things present nor things to come, nor height nor depth, nor any other created thing, shall be able to separate us from the love of God which is in Christ Jesus our Lord.*

In other words, because we are now "in Christ Jesus," there is no longer any condemnation.[93] God, who is all-powerful, cannot fail to provide the heavenly home He has promised to all those who exercise trust and faith in His Son Jesus Christ.[94]

Although God's omnipotence effectively assures our salvation, the fact remains that we can live our lives here on this earth in such a way as to lose that which God's faithfulness guarantees. For

---

92 1 Peter 5:4; 2 Timothy 4:8.

93 Romans 8:1.

94 See 2 Timothy 1:12.

example, in Revelation 2:10, the Lord assures a "crown of life" only to those who remain "faithful unto death." In 1 Corinthians 4:2, the apostle Paul makes it clear that "faithfulness" is the true test of our stewardship to Christ. In his letter to the Ephesian church, Paul addresses the "saints which are at Ephesus" and the "faithful in Christ Jesus."[95] These are not two different groups. The saints are those who are faithful in Christ Jesus. The same is true at Colosse.[96] This is why Paul exhorted Christians everywhere to "continue in the faith."[97] The word of God makes it clear that eternal salvation in heaven is dependent upon our continued faithfulness to Christ.[98] "If you continue in the faith" implies that turning from the faith is certainly possible. In fact, in Galatians 5:4, the apostle Paul makes it clear that a child of God can fall from grace, something Calvinist teachers, who tout the doctrine of "once saved, always saved," flatly deny. As disciples of Christ, we are more than willing to let God be true, but every man a liar.[99] When it comes to religious truth, only God, who cannot lie,[100] is to be trusted.

In Philippians 2:12, the apostle Paul wrote, "Therefore, my beloved, as you have always obeyed, not as in my presence only, but now much more in my absence, work out your own salvation with fear and trembling." The apostle is not saying that every man is left to his own devices with regard to salvation, as if salvation were totally dependent upon man. On the contrary, salvation is, first and foremost, dependent upon the grace of God. Man, in spite

95 Ephesians 1:1.
96 Colossians 1:1.
97 Acts 14:22.
98 See Colossians 1:20-23.
99 Romans 3:4.
100 Titus 1:2.

of anything he might do, cannot, without God's unmerited favor, save himself. The provision of salvation is totally of God. Nevertheless, man, in order to be saved, is under obligation to do something. Consequently, when man does whatever it is he is required to do, he is said to be saving himself.[101] What, then, is man required to do? Quite simply, he is required to obey God! On the first Pentecost after Jesus' death, resurrection, and ascension into heaven, those who had heard and believed the gospel were required to repent and be baptized by the authority of Christ in order to have their sins remitted.[102] In other words, Christ is the author of eternal salvation unto all those who obey Him.[103] If we acknowledge Jesus as Lord and obey Him, He will save us from our past sins. In addition, in order to stay saved, we must continue to serve Him faithfully. As we do this, we are said to be working out our own salvation "with fear and trembling."[104] "For," as the next verse says, "it is God who works in you both to will and to do for His good pleasure." The Christian works out his own salvation by reverently and carefully following the Lord's preceptive will. In doing so, he "proves what is that good and perfect will of God."[105]

The idea that one cannot be cast off forever is not taught in the Scriptures. In his wise counsel to his son Solomon, David warned: "As for you, my son Solomon, know the God of your father, and serve Him with a loyal heart and with a willing mind; for the Lord searches all hearts and understands all the intent of the thoughts. If you seek Him, He will be found by you; but if you forsake Him,

---

[101] See Acts 2:40, KJV.
[102] Acts 2:38.
[103] Hebrews 5:9.
[104] Philippians 2:12.
[105] Romans 12:2.

He will cast you off forever."[106] Then, in Ezekiel 18:24, it is said: "But when a righteous man turns away from his righteousness and commits iniquity, and does according to all the abominations that the wicked man does, shall he live? All the righteousness which he has done shall not be remembered; because of the unfaithfulness of which he is guilty and the sin which he has committed, because of them he shall die." Then, in Matthew 10:22, Jesus said, "But he who endures to the end will be saved." Why did He say this? Is not the clear implication that if we do not endure we will be lost? Do Jesus' words not imply that it is possible not to endure to the end? The answer to these questions appears to be obvious: One who has been saved can fail to endure to the end and, if he does, he will be lost! This is exactly the same message Jesus taught in Matthew 24:13. For sure, Jesus was no Calvinist! In John 15:2, He said, "Every branch in Me that does not bear fruit He takes away; and every branch that bears fruit He prunes, that it may bear more fruit." In verse 6, He continues, "If anyone does not abide in Me, he is cast out as a branch and is withered; and they gather them and throw them into the fire, and they are burned." Now, does this sound like the saved cannot be lost? Again, the answer is obvious. Of course, this is exactly what the apostle Paul taught: "For if God did not spare the natural branches, He may not spare you either. Therefore consider the goodness and severity of God: on those who fell, severity; but toward you, goodness, if you continue in His goodness. Otherwise you also will be cut off."[107] The apostle Paul was not a Calvinist either! In fact, the apostle Paul was very much aware that if he did not discipline his own body and keep it under subjection that he himself could be a "castaway," and this after

[106] 1 Chronicles 28:9.
[107] Romans 11:21, 22.

having preached the gospel to others.[108] And listen to what Paul said to the church at Corinth: "Moreover, brethren, I declare to you the gospel which I preached to you, which also you received and in which you stand, by which also you are saved, if you hold fast that word which I preached to you, unless you believed in vain."[109] Paul said they heard the gospel, believed it, stood in it, and were saved by it, but that they needed to continue to hold fast, unless they had believed in vain, in which case they would, by implication, become unsaved or lost.

It is clear that the Bible does not teach Calvin's system. I could continue to cite passage after passage refuting the idea of "once saved, always saved" or "the Perseverance of the Saints," but the ones cited above are sufficient to prove Calvinism wrong.

108 1 Corinthians 9:26, 27, KJV.
109 1 Corinthians 15:1, 2.

Chapter 6

Calvinistic "Sugar-Sticks"

In this section, we are going to look at some Calvinistic "sugar-sticks" or proof-texts. Admittedly, some of these passages are a little difficult for a non-determinist. Trying to deal with these passages without having a thorough biblical understanding as to why determinism is wrong could make one feel compelled to make a misapplication of these scriptures. Nevertheless, these so-called "sugar-sticks" can be satisfactorily interpreted from a non-determinist point of view. One ought not to undertake an examination of these proof-texts without a clear understanding as to why Calvinism is anti-biblical. Therefore, if you have not already read what has been written up to this point in this study, you need to do so. Having said that, let us now proceed to an examination of these Calvinistic "sugar-sticks."

Romans 5:12, *"Wherefore, as by one man sin entered into the world, and death by sin; and so death passed upon all men, for that all have sinned"* (KJV). In the Latin translation of this passage, the Greek phrase *eph' ho* is rendered "in him," so that the last part of the passage reads, "for in him all men sinned." Therefore, in making his argument for "Original Sin," Augustine, who, as has already been pointed out, was the father of this doctrine, repeatedly made reference to this verse in his many writings, thinking it to be clear and unequivocal. Even so, in their *Commentary on Romans*, which is recognized as one of the great modern textual authorities on the book of Romans, Sanday and Headlam, on pages 133-134, wrote, "Although this expression (*eph' ho*) has been much fought over, there can now be little doubt that the true rendering is 'because.'" According to them, the Greek classical writers used this phrase to mean "on condition that." In their consideration of the idea that the apostle meant to imply, "because all sinned in Adam," they wrote: "The objection is that the words supplied are far too important to be left to be understood. If St. Paul had meant this, why did he not say so? The insertion of *in Adam* would have removed all ambiguity."[1]

Consequently, Romans 5:12 neither says nor implies that all sinned in Adam, as Augustine and, later, Luther and Calvin thought and taught. Nevertheless, this passage and its context is not easy to understand. First of all, what kind of death is under consideration in this passage? Was Paul writing about physical death or spiritual death? Most commentators seem to be in agreement that Paul is referring to spiritual death. This seems clear from his statement that death passed upon all men because all have sinned. This echoes the words of Ezekiel, who said, "The soul who sins shall die,"[2] and Paul's words in Romans 3:23, which say, "For all have sinned and fall short of the glory of God." Little children do not themselves sin, and even most Calvinists agree that this is true, therefore little children do not die spiritually. This can only mean that little children are not the subject of Romans 5:12 and 3:23, anymore than they are of Ezekiel 18:4,20, which falls within the immediate context of the statement: "Yet you say, 'Why should the son not bear the guilt of the father?' Because the son has done what is lawful and right, and has kept all My statutes and observed them, he shall surely live. The soul who sins shall die. The son shall not bear the guilt of the father, nor the father bear the guilt of the son. The righteousness of the righteous shall be upon

---

1 *Ibid.*, emphasis mine—*AT.*

2 Ezekiel 18:4, 20.

himself, and the wickedness of the wicked shall be upon himself."[3] Although Calvinism teaches that the son (viz., all the descendants of Adam) bears the guilt of the father (Adam), God says this is simply not so! Therefore, non-determinists have held that children are not in need of salvation, because if they have not sinned, they are not lost. Therefore, when Paul, referring to the atoning death of Jesus Christ, wrote "that if One died for all, then all died,"[4] the death he was speaking of was spiritual death and the "all" did not include children.

Therefore, Romans 5:12, while associating the sinful condition (i.e., spiritual death) all men share with Adam, with whom the condition first started, does not say the fallen nature of all mankind (children excluded) is inherited from Adam. Here, and elsewhere, the Bible teaches that we do not share his sin or guilt,[5] but ever since Adam, sin has spread like a cancer until all of us have sinned. Today, like in Adam's time, the entire human race shares in the same sinful condition. But, someone says, "Eve sinned first, why is she not specifically mentioned?" The answer is simple: Until Adam sinned, "all" the human race had not spiritually died; but, when Adam sinned, all mankind was fallen, and ever since that time, "all have sinned and fall short of the glory of God."[6]

Why, then, do little babies die physically? Is not this because they share the guilt of Adam? No! Little babies do not share Adam's guilt, nor the guilt of their own parents; nevertheless, they do share in the consequences of Adam's sin and, many times, the sins of their own parents. AIDS babies are a vivid reminder to us

---

3 Ezekiel 18:19, 20.
4 2 Corinthians 5:14.
5 See Romans 5:14.
6 Romans 3:23.

today that innocent babies suffer the consequences of their parents' sinful deeds. Likewise, a consequence of Adam's sin was that neither he nor any of his descendants would have access to the "tree of life" on the purely physical plane,[7] which means it is now (ever since Adam's sin) "appointed for men to die once."[8] Therefore, children die, not because they have inherited the guilt of Adam's sin, but because they, as members of the human race, share in the consequences of the human race's falleness. Some hesitate to use the word "falleness" because they are afraid it may connote a belief in Calvinism. As sensitive as I am to this position, I decided a long time ago to let the Bible, not Calvinists, dictate to me the use of biblical expressions. That man's falleness is an idea expressed in Scripture over and over again is quite clear.[9] All have sinned means all are fallen.[10] Consequently, I join my voice with that of the apostle Paul, who said: "O wretched man that I am! Who will deliver me from this body of [this self-inflicted spiritual] death? I thank God, through Jesus Christ our Lord!"[11]

Psalm 51:5, *"Behold, I was shapen in iniquity; and in sin did my mother conceive me"* (KJV). Most agree that the scribal insertion at the beginning of this psalm is correct. This means the psalm was written by David after Nathan had told him, "You are the man!"[12] Therefore, Psalm 51 is the bitter cry of one broken with guilt and pain. Now, although I realize David was a prophet, my question is this: Are all David's words in this Psalm to be taken as sober

---

7 See Genesis 3:22-24; Revelation 22:14.

8 Hebrews 9:27.

9 1 Corinthians 10:12; 1 Timothy 3:6-7; Galatians 5:4; Revelation 2:5.

10 Romans 3:23.

11 Romans 7:24, 25.

12 See 2 Samuel 12.

theological pronouncements? If you think so, then you believe that verse 4 is teaching that one can only sin against God, not man! But did not David also sin against Uriah? The answer seems obvious. Yes, David sinned against Uriah, but all sin is a personal affront to God, and He has the right to judge man for it. In other words, sin is always God's business. Therefore, when it comes to verse 5, whatever David might have been saying about his parents, he said nothing about inherited sin or "sinning in Adam."

Psalm 58:3, *"The wicked are estranged from the womb; they go astray as soon as they are born, speaking lies"* (KJV). Surely the psalmist is to be granted some "poetic license." Are we really to think that a baby, the moment it is born, begins to speak lies? The point here is not inherited total depravity, as Calvinists would like for us to believe, but the idea that it seems like almost from the time an individual is born, that is, "from his youth,"[13] he goes astray. In other words, people who are wicked usually get started very early.

Job 14:4, *"Who can bring a clean thing out of an unclean? not one"* (KJV). A woman who gives birth to a child, having by that time reached the age of accountability, has therefore sinned, and the child to which she gives birth, upon reaching the age of accountability, will also sin. Consequently, this verse is just another way of saying that "all have sinned."[14]

Job 15:14-16, *"What is man, that he should be clean? and he which is born of a woman, that he should be righteous? Behold, he putteth no trust in his saints; yea, the heavens are not clean in his sight. How much more abominable and filthy is man, which drinketh iniquity like water?"* (KJV). Nothing said in this passage, or the one mentioned above, teaches man is born totally depraved. Furthermore, even if

13 Genesis 8:21.

14 Romans 3:23; 5:12.

this passage did teach what Calvinists try to make it teach, it would be highly suspect in that these are words spoken by Eliphaz, of whom God said, "My wrath is aroused against you and your two friends, for you have not spoken of Me what is right, as My servant Job has."[15]

Jeremiah 17:9, *"The heart is deceitful above all things, and desperately wicked: who can know it?"* (KJV). Yes, it most certainly is! Once we allow sin to enter in, our human hearts become corrupted and spiritually diseased. We can never again trust our own feelings or emotions. Consequently, many sins that are really very wicked "feel" like they are okay. In another place, Jeremiah said: "O Lord, I know the way of man is not in himself; it is not in man who walks to direct his own steps. O Lord, correct me, but with justice; not in Your anger, lest You bring me to nothing."[16] As sinners who have gone astray, we need the Lord's guidance, which is readily available in the Scriptures. This is why those of us who are in a right relationship with the Lord "walk by faith, not by sight."[17]

I know I have not dealt with all the Calvinistic "sugar-sticks," but the treatment of these ought to demonstrate that Calvinistic "sugar-sticks" are not what they may first appear to be. Many come to the wrong conclusions about these passages because they do not know how to properly interpret the Bible.[18] Being able to cite a few proof texts might make, and even keep, one a Calvinist, but learning how to rightly divide the Scriptures allows one to become, and stay, a Christian.

---

15 Job 42:7.
16 Jeremiah 10:23, 24.
17 2 Corinthians 5:7.
18 See 2 Timothy 2:15.

In the following chapters, which are designed primarily for those who are not Calvinists, but have felt the influence of Calvin's man-made doctrine on their thinking, we'll ask, and do our best to answer, the following questions: (1) What Does The Bible Really Teach About Predestination? (2) Does The Bible Teach Salvation By "Grace Through Faith" Or "By Law Through Works"? (3) Who Are The Elect, And Why? (4) Blessed Assurance: What Does The Bible Really Teach About The Perseverance Of The Saints?

Finally, we'll spend a chapter dealing with something I've dubbed "The Calvinism Versus Arminianism Hoodwink And Its Deceptive Result," which is designed to put the so-called Calvinism-Arminianism dichotomy in its proper place among the infamous religious lies perpetrated by those who, for a variety of reason, seek to "suppress the truth in unrighteousness" (Romans 1:18).

Chapter 7

What Does The Bible Really Teach About Predestination?

The Bible tells us the "Father of glory,"[1] the "Lord of glory,"[2] and the "Spirit of glory"[3] are all three involved in a great endeavor to bring "many sons to glory."[4] This plan, appropriately called the Scheme of Redemption, both originated and culminates in eternity.[5] When one reads the verses cited, it is difficult to avoid the idea that this glorious scheme is, in the mind of God, a "done deal." But not a *done deal* the way the Calvinists claim. Yes, the Greek word *proorizo*, translated in the KJV as "predestinate," does mean to "predetermine," "decide beforehand," or "foreordain."[6] However, this does not mean that God made a choice of those He would save independent of anything they would do of their own free wills, as Calvinists wrongly teach. Instead, God decreed in eternity (i.e., He predestinated) that those who were going to be saved would be conformed to the image of His Son, as Romans 8:29 says.

Contrary to the determinists' point of view, God did not choose individuals to be saved *unconditionally*. Instead, based

1 Ephesians 1:17.
2 1 Corinthians 2:8.
3 1 Peter 4:14.
4 Hebrews 2:10.
5 Romans 8:29, 30.
6 See *Strong's Concondance*.

upon His foreknowledge, He predestinated (or determined beforehand) those who would be saved *conditionally* (i.e., those who would be conformed to the image of His Son). As Paul wrote in Ephesians 1:4-5:

> *...just as He [the Father] chose us in Him [Jesus Christ] before the foundation of the world, that we should be holy and without blame before Him in love, having predestined us to adoption as sons by Jesus Christ to Himself, according to the good pleasure of His will.*

Consequently, when the divine *Logos* came to this earth as the Suffering Servant of Isaiah 53 in order to "taste death for everyone,"[7] He did so for the ultimate purpose of redeeming those who would be the "many sons" and "many brethren" of Hebrews 2:10 and Romans 8:29. And, although the Father foreknew those who would be conformed to the image of His Son, the actual work of atonement was not limited to just these individuals, for it is not now, nor has it ever been, God's desire that anyone should perish.[8] Even so, it is only those who are conformed to the image of His Son (i.e., those who are "predestined to...adoption as sons"[9]) who will eventually be saved. Concerning these, Paul wrote, "Moreover whom He predestined, these He also called; whom He called, these He also justified; and whom He justified, these He also glorified."[10]

The theological concepts of "universal salvation" and "once saved, always saved" are not taught in the Bible. However, the idea

---

7 Hebrews 2:9.
8 2 Peter 2:9.
9 Ephesians 1:5.
10 Romans 8:30.

that God knows those who are His—not just now but forever—is something that is clearly taught in the Bible.[11] In fact, it is this group (who are also known by God individually) that Paul wrote about in 2 Corinthians 3:18, where he said:

> *But we all, with unveiled face, beholding as in a mirror the glory of the Lord, are being transformed into the same image from glory to glory, just as by the Spirit of the Lord.*

In other words, as we see the glory of the Lord (i.e., the fullness of His grace and truth),[12] we are being transformed into the image of His Son.[13] Without being "conformed" or "transformed" into His image, one can neither become a Christian nor remain a Christian. This *image*, *disposition*, or *mind* to which all true Christians must be conformed is perfectly explicated by the earthly existence of our Lord and Savior Jesus Christ, and is referred to in Philippians 2:5-8. Those of us who live in the flesh, like the Word who took upon Himself flesh, must humble ourselves just as He humbled Himself. We must become obedient even unto death, just as He did.

With all this said, anyone who thinks this means that the Christian must live perfectly in order to be saved is seriously mistaken. Yes, Jesus lived perfectly sinless in all His doings,[14] and we believe it is this perfection that Jesus was referring to when He told Philip: "Have I been with you so long, and yet you have not known Me,

---

[11] 2 Timothy 2:19; cf. Luke 10:20; Philippians 4:3; Revelation 3:5; Romans 8:29, 30.

[12] John 1:14.

[13] Romans 8:29.

[14] John 8:29, 34, 46; cf. 1 John 3:5, 8, 9.

Philip? He who has seen Me has seen the Father; so how can you say, 'Show us the Father?'"[15]

And, as we have already learned, the Bible makes it clear that we must be conformed to the Lord's image; but the Bible teaches us just as clearly that the only way we can possess perfection is by the gift of righteousness through faith in Jesus Christ.[16]

Addressing this very point, Paul said to Titus:

> *But when the kindness and the love of God our Savior toward man appeared, not by works of righteousness which we have done, but according to His mercy He saved us, through the washing of regeneration and renewing of the Holy Spirit, whom He poured out on us abundantly through Jesus Christ our Savior, that having been justified by His grace we should become heirs according to the hope of eternal life.*[17]

Then, writing to the Ephesians about the same thing, Paul said:

> *But God, who is rich in mercy, because of His great love with which He loved us, even when we were dead in trespasses, made us alive together with Christ (by grace you have been saved), and raised us up together, and made us sit together in the heavenly places in Christ Jesus, that in the ages to come He might show the exceeding riches of His grace in His kindness toward us in Christ Jesus. For by grace you have been saved through faith, and that not of yourselves; it is the gift of God, not of works, lest anyone should boast.*[18]

---

15 See John 14:6-11.

16 Romans 3:21, 22; 2 Corinthians 5:21; Philippians 3:9.

17 Titus 3:4-7.

18 Ephesians 2:4-9.

These passages, if they mean anything, and they mean a lot, teach that a man isn't saved by his perfect doing (i.e., works), for under such a system, all are found wanting. With this said, it is time to notice what the Scriptures say about the righteousness of God (viz., the imputed righteousness) that is ours by "grace through the redemption that is in Christ Jesus."[19]

Sinless Perfection Vs. Imputed Righteousness

As some grudgingly admit, "walking in the light"[20] is not sinless perfection. I say "grudgingly," because after hearing a brother in Christ upbraid another for teaching that walking in the light is not sinless perfection, I talked with this individual about what I thought were his misrepresentations of the position of the one being critiqued, who was, as is too often the case, not present to defend himself. After discussing the issue for a while, I finally asked him this question: "Do you believe that walking in the light is sinless perfection?" After a long pause, he said: "No." "But," he continued, "it's dangerous for us to say so publicly because those in the pews, who are not as studied as we are, will take this and run off into Calvinism." I was both shocked and sickened by the hypocrisy and clerical superiority I saw and heard that day.

Yes, like many others, I believe some have gone too far in their interpretation of 1 John 1:5-10. In fact, some believe and teach what I think is egregious error on this passage. Even so, this does not give me or anyone else the right to misrepresent either this passage or what someone might have said about it.

---

19 See Romans 3:21-24.
20 1 John 1:7.

When we read 1 John 1:5-10, it is clear that God is not just "in the light," as verse seven points out, but "God is light," as verse five indicates. This means that righteousness is not a standard by which God is to be judged—instead, God is the standard! Sinful creatures that we are, we will always find ourselves coming up short of this standard.[21] It is true that when the Light of the world[22] took upon Himself flesh and lived among us He was perfectly righteous in all His thinking, saying, and doing. Nevertheless, as we, His followers, "walk in the light as He is in the light," this will not be a perfect walk—we will make mistakes; we will sin. To deny this is to call God a liar.[23] However, when we do sin—and again the Bible says we will—we will confess our sin, if we are truly "walking in the light"(v. 9), and ask the Lord to forgive us, and then confidently trust that He has, in fact, done so.[24]

Now, although no flesh has any cause to glory in His presence,[25] because all have sinned and fallen short of the glory of God,[26] as we become obedient to Christ, we do receive a "righteousness of God" that is not our own.[27] The New Testament refers to this as imputed righteousness.[28] Some—the Calvinists are notorious for this—have mistakenly thought that the righteousness imputed to the obedient believer entails Jesus' perfect life. In other words, many wrongly think that God no longer sees the sins of His saints when He views them. According to this doctrine,

---

21 See Romans 3:20; Galatians 2:16.

22 John 1:9; 9:5.

23 1 John 5:10.

24 Verse 9; see also 1 John 5:14, 15.

25 1 Corinthians 1:29.

26 Romans 3:23.

27 Romans 1:17; 3:21, 22; 10:3; 2 Corinthians 5:21; Philippians 3:9.

28 See Romans 4:11, 23-25.

when God looks at Christians, He only sees the perfect doings of Jesus while He was here on this earth—perfect doings which have now been imputed or accredited to us. This view is completely false! The righteousness imputed to the obedient believer is not derived directly from the Lord's perfect life. Instead, our imputed righteousness derives from the fact that Jesus' sacrificial death satisfied the debt we owed for our sins.[29] In this way, according to Romans 4:5, and this way only, we, "the ungodly," have been justified.[30] Thus, if God has so justified us, who is it that can bring a charge against God's elect and make it stick?[31]

But, and here is another critical point, although we are no longer under a system of perfect law-keeping for justification, we are "under law toward Christ."[32] As we follow Him as absolute Lord of our lives,[33] we are under obligation to be conformed to His image while He was here on earth so we can one day be conformed to His glorified image in heaven.[34] As we do so, we become involved in those works (i.e., righteous deeds) God previously prepared for us: "For we are His workmanship, created in Christ Jesus for good works, which God prepared beforehand that we should walk in them."[35] By doing so, we are able to "prove what is that good and acceptable and perfect will of God."[36] In fact, the Bible teaches that the Lord redeemed us from "every lawless deed" and purified us as His own special people that we might be "zealous for good

---

29 Romans 5:18.

30 Acts 13:39; Romans 3:24; Galatains 2:16; Titus 3:4-7.

31 Romans 8:33.

32 1 Corinthians 9:21.

33 Acts 2:36; Ephesians 4:5; Colossians 2:6.

34 Romans 8:29.

35 Ephesians 2:10.

36 Romans 12:2.

works."[37] These good works reflect the glory of God, just as Jesus of Nazareth reflected the glory of God in the works He performed while here on this earth.

Today, as we develop the mind of Christ, we reflect God's glory. Although the reflection of this glory is not perfect, as it was in the case of Jesus of Nazareth, it is glorious nevertheless. Beholding as in a mirror the glory of the Lord, we "are being transformed into the same image from glory to glory, just as by the Spirit of the Lord."[38] Notice that Paul wrote, "from glory to glory." We believe this expression means that as we follow Jesus as Lord, we are being transformed from the glory we now reflect in Christ to the glory we will eventually have in heaven. Now, neither this passage nor any others in the Bible teach that once we have been saved from our past sins by our obedience to Christ, we will always be saved. On the contrary, like Jesus, we too must be faithful unto death.[39] The Bible teaches that a child of God can be eternally lost.[40] At the same time, the Bible teaches that the same foreknowledge that allowed God to know His plan for redeeming man would not fail,[41] is the same foreknowledge that allowed Him to know beforehand that "many sons" would be brought "to glory" through His Son, Jesus Christ.[42] We believe that the "to glory" in this verse is equivalent to the "to glory" of 2 Corinthians 3:18. Consequently, it refers to the eternal glory that we will one day share with our glorified

---

37 Titus 2:14.

38 2 Corinthians 3:18.

39 Revelation 2:10.

40 Hebrews 10:26-31; 2 Peter 2:20-22; Revelation 3:5.

41 Acts 2:23.

42 Hebrews 2:10.

Lord.[43] These passages, of course, refer to the glorified human body (i.e., the "it" of 1 Corinthians 15:42-44) of which Jesus now partakes and which we, if we remain faithful unto death, will one day share.

Jesus, The Man, The Firstborn Among Many Brethren

Contrary to what some among us appear to think, Jesus did not quit being a man when He returned to heaven, but even now continues in heaven as a "man"[44] who, as our Mediator, lives to make intercession for us.[45] In this regard, it is interesting to note that Jesus, in Colossians 1:18, is referred to as the "beginning, the firstborn from the dead." "Beginning" here, I think, has reference to Jesus being the "Beginning of the creation of God,"[46] which is not referring to the old creation, which the Lord, as *Logos*, was very much involved in, but the new creation which exists only in connection with Christ.[47] Therefore, I believe this expression (i.e., "the beginning") refers specifically to His *position* as the "firstborn from the dead," which, in this case, means not only preeminence but also first in occurrence.

Jesus' resurrection was the first ever of its kind. That is, He is the only one who has been raised from the dead, never to die again.[48] But the time is coming when His saints will be resurrected

43 Romans 8:18-23; 2 Corinthians 4:17-5:5; Philippians 3:20, 21; Colossians 3:4; 1 Peter 5:1-4, 10.

44 1 Corinthians 15:48; 1 Timothy 2:5; Hebrews 10:12, 13.

45 Romans 8:34; Hebrews 7:25.

46 Revelation 3:14.

47 2 Corinthians 5:17; Galatians 6:15.

48 Acts 13:34; Romans 6:9.

and glorified as well.[49] Therefore, Jesus' resurrection and glorification may be viewed as the beginning of the "new heavens and the new earth" of 2 Peter 3:13. The process,[50] which will be accomplished when death has been totally destroyed by the resurrection of all the dead and the glorification of those justified by the precious blood of our Lord, has already begun! In His revelation to John, the Lord from heaven says: "Do not be afraid; I am the First and the Last. I am He who lives, and was dead, and behold, I am alive forevermore. Amen. And I have the keys of Hades and of Death."[51]

Without The Resurrection, We Have Absolutely No Hope

Jesus' resurrection is not only the beginning point of God's new creation; it is actually the very foundation of it. The power of His endless, indestructible, or indissoluble life, according to Hebrews 7:16, is the life upon which all life depends.[52] It infuses into our souls, sustains a living church in the midst of a lost and dying world, and offers hope for the new creation to come.[53] It is this the apostle Paul refers to as, "the power of His resurrection."[54] It does not surprise us, then, that in the midst of a description of the nature of the resurrected body, Paul refers to Jesus as the second and

---

[49] See again Philippians 3:20, 21.

[50] See Romans 8:29, 30.

[51] Revelation 1:17, 18.

[52] John 5:21, 26; 14:6; Acts 3:15; Galatians 2:20.

[53] cf. Acts 23:6; 1 Corinthians 15:19; Ephesians 1:17-22; Colossians 1:5.

[54] Philippians 3:10.

last Adam.[55] Jesus, our elder brother,[56] as the result of His resurrection, is the beginning of a new family that, unlike those of the first Adam, will be like Him. When we are raised, we will bear His likeness, "that He might be the firstborn among many brethren."[57] Again, this is the reason for our hope.[58] Consequently, at this very moment, "...we all, with unveiled face, beholding in a mirror the glory of the Lord, are being transformed into the same image from glory to glory, just as by the Spirit of the Lord."[59] In 2 Corinthians 4:3-6, Paul said it this way:

> *But even if our gospel is veiled, it is veiled to those who are perishing, whose minds the god of this age has blinded, who do not believe, lest the light of the gospel of the glory of Christ, who is the image of God, should shine on them. For we do not preach ourselves, but Christ Jesus the Lord, and ourselves your bondservants for Jesus' sake. For it is the God who commanded light to shine out of darkness, who has shone in our hearts to give the light of the knowledge of the glory of God in the face of Jesus Christ.*

As we conclude this section of our study, it should be pointed out that the resurrection of Jesus Christ is the guarantee of the judgment that will one day take place upon all those who reject Him, for God "...has appointed a day on which He will judge the world in righteousness by the Man whom He has ordained. He has given assurance of this to all by raising Him from the dead."[60]

---

55 1 Corinthians 15:45-49.
56 Galatians 4:4-7; Hebrews 2:10, 11; 12:1-8.
57 Romans 8:29.
58 1 Peter 1:3; 3:15.
59 2 Corinthians 3:18.
60 Acts 17:31.

"Knowing, therefore, the terror of the Lord, we persuade men."[61] Finally, with Peter, we say:

> *But the day of the Lord will come as a thief in the night, in which the heavens will pass away with a great noise, and the elements will melt with fervent heat; both the earth and the works that are in it will be burned up. Therefore, since all these things will be dissolved, what manner of persons ought you to be in holy conduct and godliness, looking for and hastening the coming of the day of God, because of which the heavens will be dissolved, being on fire, and the elements will melt with fervent heat? Nevertheless we, according to His promise, look for new heavens and a new earth in which righteousness dwells.*[62]

---

[61] 2 Corinthians 5:11a.

[62] 2 Peter 3:10-13.

Chapter 8

Does The Bible Teach Salvation "By Grace Through Faith" Or "By Law Through Works"?[1]

In Romans 1:16 and 17, the apostle Paul wrote:."For I am not ashamed of the gospel of Christ, for it is the power of God to salvation for everyone who believes, for the Jew first and also for the Greek." He concluded with, "For in it the righteousness of God is revealed from faith to faith; as it is written, 'The just shall live by faith.'"

When Paul mentions the gospel in the book of Romans, his main concern is not the difference between sin and salvation. Instead, his primary purpose is to contrast the two possible ways of salvation: either by grace through faith, or by law through works.

---

[1] Over the years I have read extensively behind Jack W. Cottrell, a prolific writer and professor of theology at Cincinnati Bible Seminary. If you are not acquainted with his *What the Bible Says about God the Creator*, *What the Bibles Says about God the Redeemer*, and *What the Bible Says about God the Ruler* series, you have missed out on some great studies of God's word. Much of this material has now been incorporated into his newest book, a systematic theology, called *The Faith Once for All: Bible Doctrine for Today*, College Press, 2002. I readily acknowledge that much that is written here is attributable to having read and studied Cottrell—a reading and study I would highly recommend to anyone. Although what I have written here ultimately represents my own thoughts, and I alone am responsible for them, to separate, at this stage of my life, my thoughts, or even prose, from Cottrell's would be most difficult.

Thus, in theory, at least, there are two roads to God. Even so, Paul's point is that one of these roads (viz., works of law) has been thoroughly and permanently blocked by our sin. Try as we might, we can never get right with God by personal righteousness and law-keeping, "for all have sinned and fall short of the glory of God" (Romans 3:23).

Consequently, all of us have failed to keep God's law perfectly. But praise be to God, He has not left us to perish. Instead, He has graciously provided an alternative route, which is FAITH—the only genuine road to God, and the only way to salvation for sinners. So, to understand just what it means to be "saved by grace through faith"[2] and to be "heirs of grace,"[3] one must understand the difference between law and grace.

Law vs. Grace

The Bible places the two systems of law and grace in sharp contrast to each other. As was previously noted, John says:

> *And of His fullness we have all received, and grace for grace. For the law was given through Moses, but grace and truth came through Jesus Christ.*[4]

In complete agreement with John, Paul warns, "You have become estranged from Christ, you who attempt to be justified by law; you have fallen from grace."[5] He says of Christians that we are "not under law but under grace."[6] "Under law" is a phrase that

---

2 Ephesians 2:8.
3 1 Peter 3:7; Titus 3:7.
4 John 1:16, 17.
5 Galatians 5:4.
6 Romans 6:14.

describes the state of every person at the beginning of his life. God is the God of "law and order." He created the universe to operate according to natural law, and for his human creatures to live according to moral law. When a person's moral consciousness develops, he is confronted with God's moral law, either by general revelation (viz., nature[7]) or special revelation (i.e., the Bible). If one remains within a system or framework of law, then on judgment day he will be judged according to the rules or terms of law. These rules may be stated quite succinctly:

If we keep the law, we will escape the penalty.

If we break the law, we will suffer the penalty.

In Deuteronomy 30:19, Moses said:

I call heaven and earth as witness today against you, that I have set before you life and death, blessing and cursing; therefore choose life, that both you and your descendants may live.

This is the way law operates. As long as we are under law, we must realize that these are the rules that apply to us. If we keep God's law, we escape the penalty of Hell. Thus, it is possible, at least theoretically, to be justified by our perfect works in obedience to God's commandments. However, the problem with this system is that just one sin makes us a lawbreaker and subjects us to the penalty. As James says, "For whoever shall keep the whole law, and yet stumble in one point, he is guilty of all."[8]

Paul makes this same point when he says, "For as many as are of the works of the law are under the curse; for it is written, 'Cursed

---

7 See Romans 1:18-32; 2:14, 15.

8 James 2:10.

is everyone who does not continue in all things which are written in the book of the law, to do them.'"[9]

Thus, to be saved under law (which is where we all begin), one must live an absolutely perfect life. But the terrifying reality is that "There are none righteous, no, not one."[10] "For all have sinned and fall short of the glory of God."[11] This means that as long as we remain under law, we are bound to be lost, and it is just here that the gospel is most appealing. God has provided an alternative to law—another way to be saved. It is the way of grace. It is a totally different system, and it operates according to a completely different set of ground rules.

Under grace, one approaches God for salvation on the following simple terms:

If we keep the law, we will suffer the penalty.

If we break the law, we will escape the penalty.

Thank God, then, for grace, for under such a system a lawbreaker (a sinner like you and me) may escape the penalty of eternal damnation. Therefore, "If we break the law, we will escape the penalty" is good news indeed. For in our present condition, and without God's magnificent and merciful grace, we don't stand a chance of ever making it to Heaven.

But wait a minute, one might say, isn't there something wrong with these terms? After all, why should one who keeps the law suffer the penalty, while the one who breaks the law escapes the penalty? This doesn't seem fair!, you might think, and you are right. It isn't fair, and it is not supposed to be. For if it were, it could not be

9 Galatians 3:10.
10 Romans 3:10.
11 Romans 3:23.

grace. Law, you see, is fair. But Grace, praise be to God, is much more than fair, and I'll expand on this in just a moment.

Okay, but just one more thing, you say. You can accept, even embrace with open arms, the second part of the system, that is, "If we break the law, we will escape the penalty." That's great, because that's our only hope, you say. But what about that first rule: "If we keep the law, we will suffer the penalty"? Surely this is going much too far! How can that be grace, you are thinking, and who would ever agree to such a thing?

Grace, Praise Be To God, Isn't Fair

It is just here that we must understand that grace is different from our ordinary way of thinking, for it does not fit within the framework of law and justice, or even our sense of fairness. This is especially true of the statement, "If we keep the law, we will suffer the penalty." Nevertheless, this is the very element of grace that makes it grace. For without this provision, the other one—the one that says, "If we break the law, we will escape the penalty," would not be possible. After all, to whom does the first provision apply? In other words, who has kept the law perfectly? Only one person: Christ, the sinless Jesus of Nazareth. But even though He kept the law perfectly, He suffered the penalty. And why? Because, only the demands of grace could nail our spotless Lord to the cruel cross of Calvary, for in His sinless death He suffered the full penalty of the law in our place, and thus made it possible for us, as actual law-breakers, to escape the penalty. Again, praise God for His magnificent grace and mercy!

This system of grace is summed up perfectly in 2 Corinthians 5:21, which says, "For He made Him who knew no sin to be sin for us, that we might become the righteousness of God in Him." In other words, Jesus took our sins upon Him and paid the price so that we could receive an imputed righteousness (i.e., a righteousness graciously put to our account by a God who loved us in spite of our sins), "even the righteousness of God which is through faith in Jesus Christ."[12] And as Ephesians 2:8-9 says, "For by grace you have been saved through faith, and that not of yourselves; it is the gift of God, not of works, lest anyone should boast."

Here, then, is the choice: We can remain under law, to our certain condemnation; or we can accept the free gift of grace and become "heirs of God and joint heirs with Christ."[13] Of course, *choice* is not something Calvinists think we human beings actually have. But if we do have free-will choices to make, and the Bible says we do, then the false system of Calvinism is defeated. This is why Calvinists do everything in their power to try and explain away the clear teachings of Scripture.

But one thing must be clear. In distinguishing between law and grace, I am not talking about the difference between the Old Testament and the New Testament. What I've said here about law applies to any form of God's law in any age. No one was ever saved by perfectly keeping the Old Testament, or law of Moses. And by the same token, no one is saved by perfectly keeping the New Testament commandments either. Why? Because once a person has sinned, law, in any form, is unable to save him. Remember, the law says, "If we break the law, we will suffer the penalty." What, then, was the purpose of the Old Testament law? Paul says it was given "because of transgressions" until the "Seed" (viz., Jesus Christ) should come.[14] This tells us that Moses' law was given to help control man's sinful tendencies, and to make it clear, ultimately, that

---

12 Romans 3:22a.

13 Romans 8:17.

14 See Galatians 3:19.

every man is a sinner and thus cannot be saved by perfect law-keeping. Paul says, "for by the law is the knowledge of sin."[15] Thus, "the law was our tutor to bring us to Christ, that we might be justified by faith."[16] In other words, as our schoolmaster, the law taught us that Christ, as the manifestation of God's grace, was the only source of salvation. This means that the law itself was never intended to be the instrument of salvation.

In Galatians 3:21-25, Paul wrote:

> *Is the law then against the promises of God? Certainly not! For if there had been a law given which could have given life, truly righteousness would have been by the law. But the Scripture has confined all under sin, that the promise by faith in Jesus Christ might be given to those who believe. But before faith came, we were kept under guard by the law, kept for the faith which would afterward be revealed. Therefore the law was our tutor to bring us to Christ, that we might be justified by faith. But after faith has come, we are no longer under a tutor.*

This means that Old Testament saints who were saved were saved by grace just like we are today. The New Testament's favorite example of this truth is Abraham. In fact, Paul uses Abraham to prove his main point, which is that "a man is justified by faith apart from the law."[17] The full blessings of salvation and eternal life were offered to Abraham and his family, and through him to all peoples of the earth: "I will bless those who bless you, and I will curse him who curses you; and in you all the families of the earth shall be

---

15 Romans 3:20.

16 Galatians 3:24.

17 Romans 3:28.

blessed"[18]; "And the Scriptures, foreseeing that God would justify the nations by faith, preached the gospel to Abraham beforehand, saying, 'In you all the nations shall be blessed.' So then those who are of faith are blessed with believing Abraham"[19]; "There is neither Jew nor Greek, there is neither slave nor free, there is neither male nor female; for you are all one in Christ Jesus. And if you are Christ's, then you are Abraham's seed, and heirs, according to the promise."[20]

Now, how did Abraham receive his glorious inheritance? How did anyone else in the Old Testament era receive it? How does anyone receive it in the New Testament age? Paul says the inheritance does not depend on perfect law-keeping, but on God's promise: "For if the inheritance is of the law, it is no longer of promise; but God gave it to Abraham by promise."[21] Thus, Abraham received the blessing through faith in God's promise: "For the promise that he would be the heir of the world was not to Abraham or to his seed through the law, but through the righteousness of faith"[22]; "And [Abraham] believed in the Lord, and He accounted it to him for righteousness."[23]

The apostle Paul makes it clear that the inheritance of grace is shared by all in the family of Abraham. Who is it, then, who belongs to Abraham's family? Those who, like Abraham, believe in

---

18 Genesis 12:3.

19 Galatians 3:8, 9.

20 Galatians 3:28, 29.

21 Galatians 3:18.

22 Romans 4:13.

23 Genesis 15:6, quoted in Romans 4:3; Galatians 3:6; and also mentioned in James 2;23.

(that is, they trust in) the promise of God—that is, Abraham is "the father of all who believe."[24] As Paul said in Galatians 3:26-29:

> *For you are all sons of God through faith in Christ Jesus. For as many of you as were baptized into Christ have put on Christ. There is neither Jew nor Greek, there is neither slave nor free, there is neither male nor female; for you are all one in Christ Jesus. And if you are Christ's, then you are Abraham's seed, and heirs according to the promise.*

Saved By Grace Through Faith

In Ephesians 2:8-9, the Scriptures say, "For by grace you have been saved through faith, and that not of yourselves; it is the gift of God, not of works, lest anyone should boast." Therefore, how sad it is to see Christians who continue to think like the Pharisee in Luke 18:9-14:

> *Two men went up to the temple to pray, one a Pharisee and the other a tax collector. The Pharisee stood and prayed with himself, "God I thank You that I am not like other men—extortioners, unjust, adulterers, or even as this tax collector. I fast twice a week; I give tithes of all that I possess." And the tax collector standing afar off, would not so much as raise his eyes to heaven, but beat his breast, saying, "God be merciful to me a sinner!" I tell you, this man went down to his house justified rather than the other; for everyone who exalts himself will be abased, and he who humbles himself will be exalted.*

---

[24] Romans 4:16.

On Judgment Day, I am afraid some, like the Pharisee, will appeal to keeping the commandments for entry into heaven. On the other hand, the true child of God will appeal to his trust (I'm talking "faith" here) in God's promise of salvation through the grace manifested in connection with the precious blood of the Savior, Jesus Christ. Therefore, and contrary to what Calvinists think, I realize, and am thankful, that our salvation depends not on our weaknesses, but on God's strength instead. In other words, our salvation does not depend upon our ability to keep law perfectly, but on God's ability to save us by faith as He promised. When we realize this, we can truly begin to live under grace as our most loving Heavenly Father surely intended:

> *Therefore, having been justified by faith, we have peace with God through our Lord Jesus Christ, through whom we have access by faith into this grace in which we stand, and rejoice in hope of the glory of God.*[25]

But Not By "Faith Alone"

Notice that neither the salvation of Ephesians 2:8, nor the justification of Romans 5:1, are through or by "faith alone," as Calvinists assert. Luther, Calvin *et al.* were wrong when they argued that "faith alone" is what these passages were really saying. In other words, these were never more than bold assertions by these men, which means that all such thinking must be categorized with the "doctrines of men" so clearly condemned in the Bible.[26] In point of fact, the Bible makes it quite clear that we are not saved by faith alone: "What does it profit, my brethren, if someone says he has

---

[25] Romans 5:1.

[26] See Matthew 15:19; Mark 7:7; and Colossians 2:22.

faith but does not have works? Can faith save him?"[27]; "Thus also faith by itself, if it does not have works, is dead"[28]; "But do you not know, O foolish man, that faith without works is dead?"[29]; "Do you see that faith was working together with his works, and by works faith was made perfect?"[30]; "You see then that a man is justified by works, and not by faith only"[31]; "For as the body without the spirit is dead, so faith without works is dead also."[32]

This is why Martin Luther thought the book of James to be "a right strawy epistle," questioning whether a book of such inferior worth even belonged in the New Testament. That is, *if you don't like it, get rid of it*. Yes, I know he thought the epistle of James contradicted what he believed Paul to have taught in his epistles—namely, that one is saved or justified by "faith alone," but as we've seen in this study, Paul never taught any such thing. And if Luther had been willing to honestly consider what James wrote by inspiration, he could have come to the correct understanding that Paul and James were not contradicting one another at all. Salvation is not by "faith alone," and the Bible clearly says so.[33] Therefore, the doctrine of "faith only" was the figment of Luther's very fertile imagination, and the same holds true for Calvin and many others in Protestantism's cohort. Again, neither Paul nor any of the New Testament writers ever taught salvation by faith alone, and I challenge anyone to prove conclusively from the Scriptures that they did.

---

27 James 2:14.
28 James 2:17.
29 James 2:20.
30 James 2:22.
31 James 2:24.
32 James 2:26.
33 See James 2:24.

Actually, Paul And James Are Very Much In Harmony

The fact is, and this is going to surprise many who hold to the Calvinist doctrine, the Faith Only doctrine is just as dead in the book of Romans as it is in the epistle of James. In Romans 1:5 (and the emphases in these following verses is mine—AT), Paul wrote, "through whom [speaking of Jesus Christ] we have received grace and apostleship for **obedience to the faith** among all nations for His name." In Romans 16:25-27, he wrote:

> *Now to Him who is able to establish you according to my gospel and the preaching of Jesus Christ, according to the revelation of the mystery which was kept secret since the world began but now has been made manifest, and by the prophetic Scriptures has been made known to all nations, according to the commandment of the everlasting God, for* **obedience to the faith**—*to God, alone wise, be glory through Jesus Christ forever. Amen.*

The faith under discussion here, in my opinion, is objective faith, that is to say, "the objective standard"—namely, the gospel of Jesus Christ.[34] Therefore, the obedience spoken of here is the obedience from the heart,[35] and obedience that is always the demonstration of biblical faith (viz., the "saving faith" that is depicted so many places in God's Word).

Saving Faith Is A Faith That Works

But what, someone might ask, is saving faith? Well, it is certainly more than mental assent, for we are told that some of the

---

[34] See Jude 3.
[35] See Romans 6:17.

Jewish leaders "believed in" Jesus, but would not, when all was said and done, confess Him "lest they be put out of the synagogue."[36] Consider, then, that in Romans 10:10, Paul said, "For with the heart one believes to righteousness, and with the mouth confession is made to salvation." Again, in Hebrews 11:6, it is said, "But without faith it is impossible to please Him, for all who come to God must believe that He is, and that He is a rewarder of those who diligently seek Him." In other words, saving faith does not just give mental assent to God's existence, but it further involves the disposition or willingness to both *trust in* and *rely upon* the object of one's belief. Thus, saving faith is not just knowing there is a God who loves us and has sent His only begotten Son into this world to die for us—although it certainly includes all this; but more than this, what makes it truly saving faith is a *trust in* and *reliance upon* Jesus Christ as Lord of one's life. What this means is that without the faith that makes Jesus Lord, and this is a faith that is willing to obey, there can be no real salvation.

The Importance Of Obedience

Speaking of Jesus Christ, Hebrews 5:9 says: "And having been perfected, He became the author of eternal salvation to all who obey Him." Then in Romans 6:17-18: "But God be thanked that though you were slaves of sin, yet you obeyed from the heart that form of doctrine to which you were delivered. And having been set free from sin, you became slaves of righteousness." In 1 Peter 1:22a, the Bible says, "Since you have purified your souls in obeying the truth through the Spirit." Then in 2 Thessalonians 1:7b-8, it says, "...when the Lord Jesus is revealed from heaven with His

[36] John 12:42.

mighty angels, in flaming fire taking vengeance on those who do not obey the gospel of our Lord Jesus Christ."

But Where Does Such Saving Faith Come From?

In answering this question, Calvinists, who believe that unregenerated man is totally depraved and completely unable to respond positively to the gospel by faith, believe faith is given directly by God in some "better felt than told experience." On the other hand, the Bible, in Romans 10:14-17, says:

> *How then shall they call on Him in whom they have not believed? And how shall they believe in Him of whom they have not heard? And how shall they hear without a preacher? And how shall they preach unless they are sent? As it is written: "How beautiful are the feet of those who preach the gospel of peace, Who bring glad tidings of good things!" But they have not all obeyed the gospel. For Isaiah says, "Lord, who has believed our report?" So then faith comes by hearing, and hearing by the word of God. But I say, have they not heard? Yes indeed: "Their sound has gone out to all the earth, and their words to the ends of the world."*

Unregenerated man, although he is certainly sin-sick and morally depraved, is not totally depraved and, therefore, unable to respond to the gospel invitation, as Calvinists think. Consequently, the Bible, over and over, calls upon man to obey the gospel and, by so doing, "save [himself] from this untoward generation."[37] But Calvinists cannot allow such a thing, for they believe that if unregenerated man can respond in such a fashion, this would have

---

[37] Acts 2:40, KJV.

man working out his own salvation,[38] which would somehow denigrate the sovereignty of God. This, Calvinists claim, would be to admit that man could somehow earn salvation. No, no, no! Man, who is a sinner, *cannot do anything to earn salvation*. But he can, and must, the Bible teaches, render obedience to the gospel of Jesus Christ in order to be saved.

In contrast with Calvinism, the Bible teaches that sin-sick man is not totally depraved and, therefore, absolutely unable to obey the gospel. Instead, the gospel is to be preached to all men and women everywhere—men and women who the Bible describes as being dead in sin.[39] This means that although their thinking is distorted and depraved, it is not *totally* distorted nor depraved, as Calvinists teach. On the contrary, those who are dead in their sins can, upon hearing the gospel, render obedience to it in faith and repentance, both of which clearly require free moral agency.

For example, in Colossians 2:11-14, Paul wrote:

> *In Him you were also circumcised with the circumcision made without hands, by putting off the body of the sins of the flesh, by the circumcision of Christ, buried with Him in baptism, in which you also were raised with Him through faith in the working of God, who raised Him from the dead. And you, being dead in your trespasses and the uncircumcision of your flesh, He has made alive together with Him, having forgiven you all trespasses, having wiped out the handwriting of requirements that was against us, which was contrary to us. And He has taken it out of the way, having nailed it to His cross.*

---

38 See Philippians 2:12.

39 See 1 Thessalonians 2:1; Ephesians 2:5.

Notice that this passage flies in the face of Calvinistic dogma. The individuals in this passage had heard the gospel and had obeyed it, thus they were raised up to walk in "newness of life," as Romans 6:4b calls it, or "alive," as it is referred to here. Before being "raised," these had been "dead in [their] trespasses." This is to say that before being raised and made alive, they were exercising themselves positively toward the gospel, and this while being dead in their sins, which is completely at odds with the think-sos of Calvinists.

Calvinists would have those mentioned above *already* raised and made alive when the inspired apostle says they were *still* dead in their trespasses. Notice that in obeying the gospel these sinners had been able to put off the "body of the sins of the flesh" by the circumcision of Christ which, in the immediate context, is described as being "buried with Him in baptism, in which [they] were also raised with Him through faith in the working of God." Thus, if this were the only passage in the Bible that refutes Calvinism, and it isn't, then it would be sufficient to show that Calvinism's teachings on this are contrary to the truths taught in God's word.

Chapter 9

Who Are The Elect, And Why?

Let me answer the questions in the above title like this: If you are not yet one of God's elect, you can be, if you so desire. All you need to do is render obedience to Jesus Christ as the Lord of your life by *believing*, *repenting*, *confessing*, and *being baptized* in order to have your sins remitted. In doing so, you are washed with the precious blood of Jesus and raised up to walk in newness of life—a new creature, if you will—truly born again and a member of "God's elect."[1]

Calvinists scoff at such statements. Why? Because, such would make God amenable to man's will, they claim, and a God subject to man's will could not be the Sovereign of the universe. Consequently, it behooves one to know who's right here, and the only way one can hope to know this is by focusing on what the Bible actually says about it.

Although the Bible uses the term "elect" in a variety of ways, it *never* uses it to indicate a select group who *alone* have been predestinated (according to the Calvinist definition of this term) to salvation. This statement is, no doubt, shocking to those who adhere to the *Westminster Confession of Faith*, for it says, "By the decree of God, for the manifestation of His own glory, some men and angels are predestinated unto everlasting life, and others foreordained to everlasting death."[2] In other words, although Calvinists define the

---

1 See Romans 8:33 and Titus 1:1 for the use of this term.

2 Chapter III, paragraph 3.

"elect" as a select group whom God has, from "eternity past," appointed to salvation and, conversely, all others are predestined to inescapable damnation, the Bible teaches no such doctrine. In fact, even Calvin seemed to have difficulty with the concept, for he wrote, "The decree, I admit, is dreadful; and yet it is impossible to deny that God foreknew what the end of man was to be before he made him, and foreknew, because he had so ordained by his decree."[3]

According to Calvin, God, because He is Sovereign, decreed everything that would ever happen, from the fall of Adam to the ultimate consigning of billions to a Devil's hell. Nevertheless, and in direct contradiction to what Calvin believed and taught, the Scriptures make it clear that God is *not willing* that any—not one—should perish.[4] Jesus shed His blood for "all" men,[5] not just a few selected ones ("the Elect"), as Calvin argued. That this is the essence of what Jesus taught is made clear by His words recorded in John 3:16, which say:

> *God so loved the world that He gave His only begotten Son, that whoever believes in Him should not perish but have everlasting life.*

That this is, undoubtedly, one of the most loved and quoted passages in the Bible cannot be safely denied. But at the same time, and most unfortunately, John 3:16 remains one of the most misunderstood and misrepresented verses in the Bible. Many who cherish this passage have little understanding of what it actually teaches. It is not my intention to examine every word in this verse,

---

3 *Institutes of the Christian Religion*, 1998 edition, Book III, Chapter xxiii, Section 7.

4 See 2 Peter 3:9; 1 Timothy 2:3, 4.

5 See 2 Corinthains 5:14, 15.

although that would be an excellent study in itself.[6] What I want to do is concentrate on the exegesis of two expressions: "the world" and "whosoever believes in Him."

"...the world..."

The Greek word translated world is *kosmos*. Although this word, in its literal sense, means the universe or the earth, it sometimes is used to refer to the *people* in all the world. As Wayne Jackson points out in the article referred to in the footnote below, "this is a figure of speech known as metonymy; in this case, the container is put for the contents, i.e., the world stands for its inhabitants." Consequently, this expression reflects God's love for all mankind, not just an elect few, as the Calvinists want us to believe. As we have already learned in this study, such a claim is completely untrue, and this is exactly what this verse teaches. As John the baptizer said, Jesus of Nazareth is the Lamb of God who "takes away the sin of the world."[7]

Yes, it is perfectly Scriptural to believe that, in the end, it is *only* the elect who will be saved. But one must keep in mind that the elect mentioned in the Scriptures are not the ones described by Calvinists, who they assert are chosen by God apart from anything He foreknew about them (viz., that they would, if given the opportunity, obey the gospel). Instead, the elect are those who, of there own free wills, decide to accept the offer of God's salvation in connection with His only begotten Son by rendering obedience

---

[6] For a good exegetical study of each word, see Wayne Jackson, "The Golden Text: A Study of John 3:16" in the *Christian Courier* at www.christiancourrier/articles/read/the_golden_text_a_study_of_john_316.

[7] John 1:29; 1 John 2:2.

to the gospel. This is why certain passages focus only on the elect in this regard, like Ephesians 5:25-27, which says:

> *...just as Christ also loved the church and gave Himself for it, that He might sanctify and cleanse it with the washing of water by the word, that He might present it to Himself a glorious church, not having spot or wrinkle or any such thing, but that it should be holy and without blemish.*

Even so, such concentration on God's elect does not negate, in any way, the fact that salvation is offered to anyone who is willing to "obey Him" (i.e., Christ)[8]—namely, "whosoever will" or "whosoever desires."[9]

So, although the Scriptures make it clear that God loves the whole of mankind and does not wish to see any perish,[10] He will not, despite Calvinist assertions to the contrary, stomp all over the free moral agency He chose to give to man by turning around and forcing him to irresistibly yield to His plan of salvation. Such is the Calvinist god, not the One who has revealed Himself in the Bible.

"...that whoever believes on Him..."

The "whoever believes" of this passage demonstrates, once again, the universality of God's great scheme of redemption. In other words, Christ "died for all" because "all [had] died."[11] This is why the Great Commission was addressed to the whole world and every creature in it.[12] But it is interesting to note the meaning of

8 See Hebrews 5:8, 9.
9 Mark 8:24 and Revelation 22:17.
10 See 2 Peter 3:9.
11 2 Corinthians 5:14, 15.
12 See Mark 16:15, 16.

the Greek word translated "believes" here, for it carries with it much more than the idea of mere mental assent. The word is *pisteuon*, a present tense participle, which means, literally, "the keeping on believing ones" and in the context of *pas o pisteuon eis auton* or "whoever believes on Him," as it appears in the NKJV, describes not just those who accept the historical facts about Christ, along with a willingness to trust Him as Savior, but those who keep on trusting Him by complying with those things He has commanded in His word.

In other words, those who are doing the believing in this passage and, as a result, obtain eternal life are those who exercise faith in (i.e., they trust and obey) Jesus not just for a moment in time, but every moment in time—that is, not only do they believe in Jesus, but they *keep on* believing in Him. As the lexicographer J. H. Thayer observed, the word translated "believes" in this passage is "used especially of the faith by which a man embraces Jesus, i.e., a conviction, full of joyful trust, that Jesus is the Messiah—the divinely appointed author of eternal salvation in the kingdom of God, *conjoined with obedience to Christ*," (emphasis mine—*AT*).[13]

In fact, faith (or belief) in the Bible is frequently contrasted with disobedience. For example, in John 3:36, the ASV and ESV translates *apeiteo* as "obeyeth not" or "does not obey" respectively, instead of "believeth not" or "does not believe" as does the KJV and NKJV. Consequently, the verse reads this way in the ESV, "Whoever believes in the Son has eternal life; whoever does not obey the Son shall not see life, but the wrath of God remains on him." Again, although John 3:16 attributes eternal life to those who believe in Jesus Christ, Hebrews 5:9 makes it clear that the Lord is the Author of eternal salvation to all those who obey Him. This

---

13 *Greek-English Lexicon*, 1974, page 511.

demonstrates that faith and obedience are not mutually exclusive as so many think, particularly the Calvinists. Instead, the faith that saves *includes* obedience.

With this in mind, let's take a look at a passage Calvinists are convinced is a proof-text for "faith only." In Romans 5:1, Paul wrote, "Therefore, being justified by faith, we have peace with God through our Lord Jesus Christ." When this passages is combined with what Paul wrote about faith in Romans 3:28 and 4:3, determinists are convinced that the faith under discussion is "faith *alone*." In fact, Luther was so convinced that this was the case, he actually added *allein* (alone) to his German translation of the Bible. In answering to why he did so, he said he believed it "conveys the sense of the text."[14] He even went so far as to call it, "The article upon which the church stands or falls." Calvin, of course, agreed with such thinking, and Faith Alone has become the clarion call of Protestantism, particularly those with a Calvinist bent.

However, the apostle Paul cannot be writing of the "faith alone" doctrine espoused by the Reformers, as such would contradict what James wrote in his epistle—namely, that one is not saved by faith only.[15] Yes, John 3:16 promises eternal life to him who believes, but Hebrews 5:9 just as clearly teaches that eternal salvation is given to those who *obey* the Lord. Combining these passages, it is not so hard to understand that the faith that saves, far from being just mental assent, is a faith that obeys, a faith that works.

As a matter of fact, the New Testament frequently uses "faith" as a synecdoche, which is a figure of speech where a *part* is made to stand for the *whole*. For example, in Acts 11:18, repentance is said to result in life, but most would understand that this is not saying

---

14 Luther's *Open Letter On Translating*, 1530.

15 See James 2:24.

repentance *alone* produces life. The same is true of baptism. In 1 Peter 3:21, the Scriptures teach that baptism saves us, but most people understand that this is not teaching one is saved by baptism *alone*.

Consequently, when one compares what Paul wrote in the book of Romans with his own conversion, one can know that He was not teaching that man is saved by faith alone. Acts 22:10 makes it clear that Paul believed in the Lordship of Jesus Christ while still on the Damascus road, but it was not until three days later that he enjoyed peace with God; that is, not until he got up and washed away his sins by being baptized into Christ.[16]

Biblical faith (i.e., saving faith) is the faith that lovingly works[17] to obey the Lord's requirements (or conditions, if you will) for experiencing the new birth of John 3:3-5, and it is the faith that continues to meet the requirements of God's magnificent grace[18] even until death.[19]

Who, then, are the elect? They are those who have met the conditions of God's grace, rendering obedience to the gospel, and continuing to do so, until the very end of their earthly sojourn. Are they creatures who were born totally depraved, as the Calvinists teach? No, they are creatures who, although sin-sick, can, upon hearing the gospel, render obedience to it.[20] Have they been unconditionally elected by God to be saved apart from anything they would do, as the Calvinists teach? No, their election is conditional,[21] and until and unless they meet these conditions, they will

16 See Acts 22:16; 9:18, 19; also Galatians 3:27 and Romans 6:3.

17 See Galatians 5:6.

18 See 1 John 1:9.

19 See Revelation 2:10.

20 See Acts 2:40.

21 See Mark 16:15, 16.

be lost.[22] The fact that the elect can have their names written in heaven,[23] and this from the foundation of the world,[24] speaks ***not to** some eternal decree* whereby God has foreordained they will be saved in spite of their own willingness (or not) to obey the gospel when that opportunity presents itself in time and space, ***but with** the foreknowledge* of God, which permits Him to foreordain or predestinate individuals based on what He knows they will do when given the opportunity.[25]

Further, is the salvation or atonement God offers through His Son, Jesus Christ, limited to only a select few (viz., the elect)? No, salvation is offered to all who will render obedience to Jesus Christ—namely, "whosoever will."[26] In other words, Jesus did not die *only* for the elect, as Calvinism teaches. Instead, He died for "all men."[27] Have the elect, then, been *irresistibly* drawn, as the Calvinist teach? Absolutely not! God's grace, which has appeared to all men,[28] can be resisted. If not, then all men will eventually be saved. However, the Bible teaches absolutely nothing about any kind of universal salvation. Yes, the gospel of Jesus Christ exerts a drawing power on all who hear it,[29] but the Bible clearly says this power can be resisted.[30] Does this mean, as the Calvinists teach, that the elect, *once saved, cannot be lost*? No, for the children of God (i.e., those who are collectively and individually referred to in God's word as

---

22 See 2 Thessalonians 1:8; 1 Peter 4:17.
23 See Luke 10:20 and Hebrews 12:23.
24 See Ephesians 1:4.
25 See Acts 2:23; Romans 8:29; 1 Peter 1:2.
26 See Matthew 16:25; Mark 8:34, 35; Revelation 22:17.
27 See 1 Timothy 2:4; 2 Corinthians 5:14, 15; 2 Peter 3:9.
28 See Titus 2:11.
29 See John 12:32.
30 See Acts 7:51.

the elect) can have their names blotted out of the book of life, according to Revelation 3:5; 20:12, 15; 22:19. In other words, the idea that once a person is saved he forever remains saved is not taught in the Bible. A Christian who sins and fails to meet the conditions of God's grace (by not repenting of and confessing one's sin)[31] can fall from grace, according to the necessary inference of Galatians 5:4. This doesn't have to be the case and it ought not to be the case, but that it can and may happen is the clear teaching of God's word. In fact, the perseverance of the saints is a doctrine we'll further examine in the following chapter.

A Closer Look At That Ol' "God Predestines The Plan, Not The Man" Adage

With the contrast between what the Bible teaches and what Calvinists teach firmly fixed in our minds, I want to take just a little space here at the end of this chapter to examine Ephesians 1:3-5, which is a section of Scripture Calvinists believe teaches their doctrine. In conjunction with this, I also want to examine the attempt some Christians have made to dodge or eliminate what they think are the Calvinistic implications if it is believed that the subjects of these verses, namely the "us" and "we," are actually *particular individuals* rather than the *corporate body* of believers. So, let's look at these verses:

> *Blessed be the God and Father of our Lord Jesus Christ, who has blessed us with every spiritual blessing in the heavenly places in Christ, just as He chose us in Him before the foundation of the world, that we should be holy and without blame before Him in*

---

[31] See Acts 8:22 and 1 John 1:9.

> *love, having predestined us to adoption as sons by Jesus Christ to Himself, according to the good pleasure of His will.*

No matter how one interprets this passage, it is clear that the "us" and "we" of these verses are the "elect of God."[32] The fact that they were chosen by Him "before the foundation of the world" makes it clear that this was a decision God made in eternity *before* creating our time-space continuum (some have called this "eternity past," for the lack of a better word). Thus, in order to counter what some believe to be the force of the Calvinists' argument concerning this passage (namely, the predestination of individuals to salvation in "eternity past," in conjunction with the companion idea that the future is, as a result, fixed and unalterable), many have seriously countered with the idea that the only predestination under discussion here is the predestination of a *plan*, not of the specific individuals in that plan. This is to say that the individuals who make up the elect are not known beforehand by God as individuals, and that the only thing that was foreknown by God was the plan by which He would redeem man if he did actually fall into sin.

In other words, and I have heard this idea expressed on numerous occasions, many Christians believe God did not actually know if man would sin before He created him, but knowing it was a possibility, He developed a contingency plan *just in case* (viz., the scheme of redemption). Many of those who hold to this position are not denying the foreknowledge of God, only that He can choose not to know some things. This is motivated primarily by the idea that God's absolute foreknowledge of the future, contingent, free will choices of men and women would cause the future to be determined in such a way that man's free will would be

---

[32] Romans 8:33; Titus 1:1.

forfeited. This is not, however, what these verses teach, nor is it what 1 Peter 1:2 teaches, nor Romans 8:29, nor any other passage in God's word. (Please refer to chapters 2, 3, and 4 for a more in-depth study of this issue.)

Yes, it is true that the church, as a group, is God's "chosen generation," that is, they are "the elect."[33] Consequently, when one is added to the church of Christ by rendering obedience to the gospel, there is no doubt that he or she becomes at that very moment one of God's elect. But this does not mean that predestination to salvation does not include God's actual foreknowledge of the specific individuals who make up this group, and it is most unfortunate that many Christians have thought so.[34]

In order to counter Calvinism's use of this passage, these brethren have believed it necessary to deny the clear teaching of God's word, which is simply (or perhaps not so simply) this: *God's foreknowledge and man's free will are not mutually exclusive.*[35] Nevertheless, I do want to make it as clear as I know how that one does not effectively counter Calvinism by denying the election of individuals in favor of group election. In my opinion, this just dodges the issue with a bunch of semantical gymnastics that, in the end, do not effectively counter Calvinism's use of this and other passages.

More than once I have questioned a Bible class I was teaching about the words "predestination" and "foreordination" and discovered that because these terms are considered to form the foundation of Calvinist doctrine, some think the Bible says nothing about them. But it is clear that the doctrine of predestination/foreordination/election is absolutely Scriptural. Furthermore, when these

---

33 1 Peter 2:9 and Colossians 3:12.

34 See Robert Shank, *Elect In The Son*, 1970, page 122 and Clinton D. Hamilton, *Truth Commentaries, 1 Peter*, 1995, page 352.

35 Refer to chapter 4 for a more in-depth treatment of this subject.

terms are properly understood, such form one of the most significant and satisfying teachings to be found in God's word. But mark this: when this doctrine is not taught, the whole counsel of God is being neglected, and this, Paul told us, is totally unacceptable.[36]

The Predestination Of Individuals To Salvation

When the Bible speaks of predestination/foreordination/election to salvation, it is, more often than not, referring to *specific individuals*, rather than a *corporate body* or *impersonal plan*. For example, in Romans 8:29-30, the apostle Paul mentions those who have not only been elected/predestinated/foreordained to salvation, but also *called*, *justified*, and *glorified*. This means, as was pointed out at the beginning of chapter 7, it is impossible to read what God has had to say in places like Ephesians 1:17, 1 Corinthians 2:8, 1 Peter 4:14, Hebrews 2:10, and Romans 8:29-30 without realizing that the glorious scheme of redemption, which was a plan in the mind of God before the foundation of the world, is in point of fact a "done deal." But don't get the wrong idea, here, for I am not saying that it is a *done deal* the way the Calvinists teach—no way! It's only a done deal in the sense that God decreed in eternity (i.e., He predestinated/foreordained/elected) that the individuals who were going to be saved would be conformed to the image of His Son, as Romans 8:29 so clearly teaches.

Furthermore, it needs to be understood that this conforming was *not* just limited to developing, and being transformed by, the mind of Christ,[37] *but* encompassed the whole *process* up to, and through which, Jesus was ultimately glorified and exalted in

---

36 See Acts 20:26, 27.

37 See Philippians 2:5-8.

heaven for having accomplished His Father's will while here on earth.[38] Like Jesus, we too will one day be resurrected to a *glorified* state[39] in the New Jerusalem from above.[40] This is why, then, that the Scriptures refer to Jesus as *not* being just "the head of the body, the church," *but* as being "the beginning, the firstborn from the dead, that in all things He might have the preeminence."[41] In other words, Jesus was the firstborn from the dead in relation to the "many brethren"[42] or "many sons"[43] who would render obedience to Him as their Lord and Savior and who would themselves, at His "second coming," be resurrected in/with/to a glorified, heavenly body.[44] But if God does not actually have absolute foreknowledge, then how could He have known that even one individual, of his own free will, would render obedience to the gospel? The Calvinists wrongly teach that He "knew before" only because He decreed/predestined/elected individuals to salvation *unconditionally*. But in stark contrast to this, the Bible teaches that God decreed/predestined/elected individuals to salvation *conditionally*. This means that in order to be saved one would have to meet the conditions of God's grace. It means that those who did so would be God's elect, individually and collectively.

Who, then, are God's elect? Those who, when confronted with the gospel, are willing, of their own free wills, to obey it. *Why* are they the elect? Because God, in His magnificent mercy, grace, and love, says so, that's why. *When* did He know them? He knows

---

38 See Philippians 2:9-11.

39 See 1 John 3:2; 2 Corinthians 5:1-8; 1 Corinthians 15:35-49.

40 See Revelation 3:12 and 21:2.

41 Colossians 1:18.

42 Romans 8:29.

43 Hebrews 2:10.

44 See note 37 above and 1 Thessalonians 4:13-18.

them now and in the future, for such is the meaning of a verse like 2 Timothy 2:19. But even more significantly, He even knew who they were "Before the foundation of the world."[45] *How* could He know exactly who these individuals were before any of them were even created? Because He is an awesome God[46] who "knows all things,"[47] "declaring the end from the beginning, and from ancient times things that are not yet done,"[48] and doing so simply because HE IS WHO HE IS.[49]

Finally, does God have absolute foreknowledge? Yes. Does man have free will? Yes. Do these somehow cancel each other out? No. How do I know? Simply this: the Bible tells me so.

---

45 Ephesians 1:4.

46 See Daniel 9:4.

47 1 John 3:20.

48 Isaiah 46:10a.

49 See Exodus 3:14 and John 9:58.

Chapter 10

"Blessed Assurance": What Does The Bible Really Teach About The Perseverance Of The Saints?

Do you know if you're saved right now? If the Lord came today and you stood before Him in judgment, do you think you would be saved? In other words, if you suddenly died right this moment, do you believe you'd go to heaven? If one is assured of his or her salvation, the answer to any of these questions would be, "Yes." But why do Christians, of all people, frequently try to "hem and haw" their way through questions like these? And where is the pleasure that is derived from the "blessed assurance"[1] that we sing about on Sunday throughout the rest of the days of the week? Why are some Christians so timid or even negative about their salvation?

I'll tell you one of the big reasons why: too many Christians have heard so many sermons criticizing denominational doctrine, like the Calvinists' "once saved, always saved" doctrine of the perseverance of the saints, that they have very little idea what the Bible really says about salvation and the Christian's joyous hope of persevering to the end. Nevertheless, in Hebrews 10:22 and 23, the Scriptures say: "Let us draw near with a true heart, in full assurance of hope, having our hearts sprinkled from an evil conscience and

---

[1] E. J. Crosby, "Blessed Assurance," *Hymns for Worship* (revised), 2000, page 4.

our bodies washed with pure water. Let us hold fast the confession of our hope without wavering, for He who promised is faithful." Consequently, this passage, along with others, flies in the face of the tenuous "maybes," "I hope sos," and "I don't knows" that Christians all too frequently mutter.

Yes, Christians who are not being faithful to the Lord should have no false assurance that they will persevere to the end and experience the joys of heaven. In fact, such should know that the only thing that awaits them in their present condition is "a certain fearful expectation of judgment, and fiery indignation which will devour the adversaries."[2] But if this is the actual condition of most Christians today, then in the context of the Lord's assurance to His disciples that He would speedily avenge His elect, is it any wonder that He asked, "Nevertheless, when the Son of Man comes, will He really find faith on the earth?"[3]

Let there be no doubt that the faith He mentions here is not the mental assent so many think about when they contemplate faith. You know the kind I'm talking about, the kind that says, "Oh, I believe, all right!" But do they? Do they trust in, rely upon, and obey the Father, Son, and Holy Spirit? Will they do this no matter what? If not, they do not have the faith that saves—that real nitty-gritty faith that says, "I will serve the Lord no matter what happens,"[4] for this is the only kind of faith that can "cut the mustard," if you catch my drift. It is only this kind of faith that thinks (heart, soul, and mind) like Paul in Romans 8:31-39:

> *If God is for us, who can be against us? He who did not spare His own Son, but delivered Him up for us all, how shall He not with*

---

[2] Hebrews 10:27.

[3] Luke 18:8b.

[4] See Daniel 3:17, 18.

Him also freely give us all things? Who shall bring a charge against God's elect? It is God who justifies. Who is he who condemns? It is Christ who died, and furthermore is also risen, who is even at the right hand of God, who also makes intercession for us. Who shall separate us from the love of Christ? Shall tribulation or distress, or persecution, or famine, or nakedness, or peril, or sword? As it is written: "For your sake we are killed all day long; we are accounted as sheep for the slaughter." Yet in all these things we are more than conquerors through Him who loves us. For I am persuaded that neither death nor life, nor angels nor principalities nor powers, nor things present nor things to come, nor height nor depth, nor any other created thing, shall be able to separate us from the love of God which is in Christ Jesus our Lord.

The Gospel Is More Than Supercalifragilisticexpialidocious!

So, the good news of the gospel is not just that Christ died for us, which was totally undeserved and, therefore, unbelievably magnanimous and magnificent in itself, that is "supercalifragilisticexpialidocious," but that in His resurrected state "He is also able to save to the uttermost those who come to God through Him, since He ever lives to make intercession for them,"[5] which is, if I may be permitted to say so, "absolutely super-supercalifragilisticeexpialidocious!" As such, Jesus, our Savior and High Priest, serves as our "Advocate with the Father," being Himself "the propitiation for our sins."[6] The term "propitiation" literally

---

5 Hebrews 7:25.
6 1 Peter 1:1, 2.

means "an offering that turns away wrath." Jack Cottrell, in his excellent book, *The Faith Once For All*, explains this nicely:

> *In pagan circles these terms [speaking of the several Greek words from which is derived "to propitiate," "a propitiation, a propitiatory offering, that propitiates God"] had the connotation of appeasing or placating angry deities. This crude pagan connotation must not be carried over into the biblical usage, however, not because the term means something different in the Bible, but because the God of the Bible is different from the false heathen deities. He is not merely a God of wrath but is also a God of love and grace who takes the initiative in providing the offering that turns away his own wrath. He does not wait in an angry pout until the anxious sinner brings him an offering he deems suitable, nor does the kindhearted Son "win over" the hard-hearted, angry Father through his death on the cross. We must not think the term "propitiation" carries only such primitive connotations. The terms are used often in the Septuagint, where they do not have "the usual pagan sense of a crude propitiation of an angry deity," something which "is not possible with the God of Israel."*[7]

This is well said, for one must not think of God and our redemption in such primitive terms. We must know that the idea involved in the use of this term is the idea of a sacrifice that turns away wrath, and if the God who has revealed Himself to man were not a God of wrath, then there would have been no need for a propitiation of that wrath. That Jesus was, through the work He was

[7] 2002, page 265. Further note that the quoting Cottrell does here is from Leon Morris, *The Apostolic Preaching of the Cross*, 1960, page 155, with Cottrell's observation that Morris' treatment of propitiation in this volumn is simply unsurpassed.

sent here to do, which culminated in His death on the cross, the propitiation for our sins is the beginning of the good news of the gospel, as was mentioned earlier. Nevertheless, our blessed assurance and hope must not focus on His earthly work alone, for He lives *now*, in His glorified state, ever to make intercession for us as we serve Him here on this earth. Praise God for the sacrifice of His only begotten Son for us on that cruel cross of Calvary! Praise God that Jesus ever lives to make intercession for us at the right hand of the Father on high! Praise God, that Jesus, who was and is Himself God, came to this earth and lived and experienced death as a man, and that in addition to being the perfect and complete sacrifice for our sins, He is able to make sympathetic intercession for us at His Father's right hand! Indeed, praise God!

That Man Would Need Redemption Was Something Foreknown By God Before The Foundation Of The World

Jesus, the One who turns away God's wrath, is Himself God. Therefore, this is no pagan ritual, no heathen concept involved here at all. It is, instead, a scheme, a plan, conceived and designed in the mind of God before the very foundation of the world.[8] Because He is who He is, He knew *then* (in eternity) what He knows *now*—namely, "The Lord knows those who are His."[9] He knew/knows this because, as God, He has absolute foreknowledge of any and every future event or act, whether ordained by Him or not. In other words, and as has been pointed frequently in this study, God even knows the future, contingent, free will choices of His creatures. This foreknowledge is not limited, as some try to

---

8 See 1 Peter 1:20; Ephesians 1:4.

9 2 Timothy 2:19. See also Nahum 1:7 for the same idea.

argue. In point of fact, God's foreknowledge of these future, contingent, free will choices is perfect (i.e., absolute), which means there is not anything that *has* happened or *will* happen that God does not know, as He is the Lord of the *then*, *now*, and *not yet*.

Therefore, God knew before creating man that he would fall into sin and be in desperate need of a Savior. Deciding, then, that He would redeem fallen man, God, specifically the Father, chose to send the *Logos* (the divine Word) into this world that the world, by Him, might be saved, as John 3:17 points out. Did God, therefore, foreknow that man would sin? Absolutely! Did God devise a plan (or scheme) whereby fallen man could be saved? Most definitely! Did God focus on His Son's death on the cross as the pivotal point in this plan? For sure! Did He know, then, in eternity and before creating this world, who would render obedience to Christ? Yes, for this is exactly what the Bible says in Ephesians 1:4. Did He not only predestinate the plan whereby man could be saved, but the actual individuals who render obedience to the gospel under this plan? Yes, for this is the clear teaching of God's word in Ephesians 1:4, as already noted, also 1 Peter 1:2, and especially Romans 8:29 and 30, which says:

> *For whom He foreknew, He also predestined to be conformed to the image of His Son, that He might be the firstborn among many brethren. Moreover whom He predestined, these He also called; whom He called, these He also justified; and whom He justified, these He also glorified.*

As I've pointed out elsewhere in this study, in order to refute the doctrine of Calvinism, which teaches that individuals have been chosen/elected by God *unconditionally*, it is not necessary, as many think, to believe that God only predestinated the church/group/plan, but *not* the man. On the contrary, the key to not falling prey to the false, man-made system of Calvinism is to understand that God predestined the church/group/plan, *and* the man, but that He predestinated the man *conditionally*—that is, conditioned upon whether a particular person would, if given the opportunity (and such depended solely upon God's grace), render obedience to the glorious gospel of Jesus Christ.

Furthermore, for those who, of their own free wills, would render obedience to the gospel, thus having their names enrolled in the book of life,[10] to continue having their names enrolled there[11] depends upon their continued faithfulness unto death.[12] Thus, if you were looking for a theme that sums up this chapter, it would be that God *has done* and *will continue to do* His part, and with God's help, we can continue to do our part—which is to remain faithful and continue to meet the conditions of His grace—until death. As was pointed out earlier, this is not some impossible task, as some seem to think, but with God's help (i.e., with God's enabling power) man has the *capacity* to live a perfectly sinless life.

Thus, Man Does Not Have To Sin

Yes, that's right, man, although suffering from human frailties and finite limitations, does not have to sin. This is to say, there is nothing inherent in being human that causes us, forces us, or compels us to sin, although this is a very prominent idea with many. In fact, Calvinists have camped out on this idea in order to sell their false ideas to the religiously gullible. But although man is not born totally depraved today, as the Calvinists teach, all men, and this point must not be missed, have sinned and fallen short of the glory

10 See Philippians 4:3; Revelation 21:27.
11 See Revelation 3:5; 20:19.
12 See Revelation 2:10.

of God (i.e., "There is none righteous, no not one"[13]). Yes, it is true that Jesus was a man who did not sin, but it must be remembered that He was not *just* a man. He was, instead, deity incarnate and, as such, was both the placator and the One being placated. Praise God for His magnificent mercy! Thus, the cause of our ruin in connection with sin lies *totally* with us, "for all have sinned and fall short of the glory of God."[14] At the same time, the means whereby man can be saved, and this in spite of his sins, is *totally* of God, for we are all "saved by grace through faith."[15]

Does Man Live Sinlessly Perfect, Then?

The answer to this question is, "No." The only man who did live sinlessly perfect was Jesus of Nazareth. In doing so, He was the *only* man who ever deserved heaven. But instead, He paid the price that was necessary to set us free from sin, taking the penalty that was our due upon Himself, as Isaiah 53 so wonderfully pronounced many hundreds of years before Jesus actually died on that cruel cross located just outside the walled city of Jerusalem some two thousand years ago. Praise God, the Father, for the magnificent, merciful, and loving sacrifice of His only begotten Son on our behalf! Praise God, that we, by obedience to God's only begotten Son as the absolute Lord and Master of our lives, could taste that precious and everlasting life that is ours in Him because He was willing and able to taste (i.e., experience) death for each one of us! Once again, praise God!

---

[13] Romans 3:10.
[14] Romans 3:23.
[15] Ephesians 2:8, 9.

Chapter 11

Did Jesus Die Vicariously?

It grieves me that some, in their efforts to refute Calvinism, are willing to deny that Jesus actually died vicariously, or in our stead, as the word indicates. In running away from Calvinism, it is not necessary, as these think, to reject the substitutional death that the Bible, in Isaiah 53 and other places, so clearly says Jesus suffered on our behalf. But sadly, this is exactly what some Christians are doing.

The following citations are taken from separate articles written by two different Christians. I'm not naming the source for either, for it is not the *who* but the *what* that I wish to concentrate on. The first quote says:

> *In the sense of the substitution theory* [this is what he calls the vicarious death of Jesus—AT], *if Jesus, when He died on the cross, removed God's wrath against sin, satisfied divine justice, paid all our debt in our place, took our punishment for sin upon himself, became guilty with our guilt, was cursed in our stead, then Jesus has already done it all in our place. How can we be charged with anything if Jesus has already done it all? If Jesus has already taken my punishment upon himself, then I do not have to worry because my punishment was removed 2000 years ago! I cannot be held accountable for what I have done because my substitute has already taken that on himself and removed any responsibility from me!*

The second quote reads exactly like the first, with the exception of the final sentence, which says, "*The only conclusion that can be reached from the substitution position is universal salvation....or Calvinist limited atonement!*" (Italics are in the original—*AT*.) This second brother went on to say the following in the very next paragraph:

> *Some will insist that they do not believe in either universal salvation or limited atonement but believe in substitution anyway. But, they don't realize what they are saying. The Bible teaches that we must do something to have our sins removed, Mark 16:15, 16, Acts 2:38. We are righteous even as He is righteous if we do righteousness, 1 John 3:7, and are acceptable with God if we work righteousness, Acts 10:34, 35. We can escape the punishment of hell but must obey God to do so, Matthew 25:32-46. We must obey God in order to enter Heaven, Matthew 7:21-27. The very fact that we must do all these things in order to have our sins removed, be righteous and escape punishment for sin demonstrates that the substitution theory is human error and not truth. Some will say they believe in the necessity of human obedience and substitution as well. Again, they don't know what they are saying. Human obedience and the substitution theory are contradictions. This is why Calvinism virtually removes any such human effort from the process. Limited atonement, irresistible grace, and the impossibility of apostasy of Calvinism are the direct results of the substitution theory. Baptist doctrine demonstrates the same things; God provides the faith and grace, once saved you can't be lost and the number is limited to those to whom God gives the grace. And why not, if Jesus has already done everything in our place? What is there for us to do?*

I wanted to include these quotes to let the reader know that I'm not constructing straw men here.[1] It is not difficult to see that these two brothers reject the vicarious death of Jesus. That is, although they know He died in order to pay the price for our redemption, they nevertheless make it absolutely clear that they reject, as gross error, the idea that Jesus died in our stead. And they do so, once again, to refute the ol' bugaboo of Calvinism. Certainly, Calvinism needs to be rejected; but in doing so, one must not reject what the Bible clearly teaches on this or any other subject.

Rejecting The Either-Or Argument

Consequently, I categorically deny and unequivocally reject the premise that if one believes in the vicarious death of Jesus, one must either accept universalism or Calvinism, for such an either-or assumption is simply not a valid Scriptural point. The Bible teaches neither of these, and I reject them both.

Furthermore, I will trust what the Bible actually says rather than what these brethren are trying to tell me it says. As I've already indicated, I will argue, from Isaiah 53 and other passages, that Jesus did, in fact, die in our stead. And although both these aforementioned brothers castigate those who hold "the substitution theory" for coming under the influence of human reasoning and denominational think-sos, I believe it is their own thinking that reflects such enslavement.

For example, in Galatians 3:13, Paul wrote, "Christ has redeemed us from the curse of the law, having become a curse for us (for it is written, 'Cursed is everyone who hangs on a tree')." Then,

---

1 A straw man is a weak or imaginary opposition set up only to be easily refuted.

in 1 Peter 2:24, we are told that Jesus "bore our sins in His own body on the tree [i.e., the cross]." Do not these passages, when coupled with Isaiah 53, convey the idea that Jesus suffered and died in our stead? Why, then, must I, in order to be thought sound in the faith, believe that Jesus didn't die in my place?

Truth is, I don't, and the convoluted logic and attempted exegeses of these two brothers changes nothing. As I pointed out in my little book, *The Christian & Idolatry*, man seems to always get into trouble with the human analogies he tries to appropriate to God.[2] *God is not a man*. Therefore, the limitations of our human analogies cannot apply across the board to Him. When we try to make them do so, we are engaged in what the Bible calls idolatry.

I am not a universalist; nor am I a Calvinist. I am, instead, a Christian who believes what God has said in His word about *who* and *what* He is, whether I can fully understand it or not. This is true even when I can't seem to find a human analogy that completely applies to Him. One must be very careful about such things, for God and His thoughts are *infinite* and, therefore, so far above us and how we think[3] that it is just impossible for us to know everything about Him. Yes, there is plenty to know about God, but there is still plenty more that we simply do not, and cannot, know.[4]

Partly Right, But Still Very Wrong

What do I mean by the above subtitle? Simply this: Yes, Jesus was the perfect-Lamb-without-blemish sacrifice offered up for us

---

2 Allan Turner, *The Christian & Idolatry*, pages 11-15 and 30-32.

3 See Isaiah 55:8, 9.

4 See Romans 11:33 and compare it with Job 26:14.

on the cross of Calvary, as the Scriptures clearly teach. Consequently, while it is perfectly acceptable for one to preach and teach that Jesus paid the price for our sins because He was the perfectly sinless blood sacrifice for our sins, serving as the means to our redemption, it is, nevertheless, important to understand that this imagery does not fully exhaust God's description of this sacrifice.

For instance, in 2 Corinthians 5:21, Paul said, "For He made Him who knew no sin to be sin for us, that we might become the righteousness of God in Him." Now, the critics of the idea that Jesus died vicariously in our place have called "nonsense" the idea that this passage, along with others, is teaching that Jesus actually took upon Himself our sins, paying in full the price for our pardon by being "the propitiation for our sins, and not for ours only but also for the whole world."[5]

Thus, I find it most disturbing that some Christians have taken to calling "nonsense" anything taught in God's word that they happen to disagree with, whether it is this issue or some other, like the controversy over the days of Creation, or the brouhaha that manifested itself a decade or so ago over the deity-humanity of Jesus.

For example, the idea that God actually created the Universe in something approaching 144 hours is considered by some among us to be silly or ridiculous, as it contradicts the "Science" of our day. Likewise, the idea that Jesus could have been 100% God and 100% man while here on this earth was clearly thought by some among us to be absolute "nonsense." But these ideas aren't silly or nonsensical at all. In fact, they represent accurately the six-day creation taught in the Scriptures and the fully God-fully man Jesus described in the New Testament. Consequently, I don't like it one

[5] 1 John 2:2.

bit when I hear Christians calling nonsense, silly, or ridiculous things I can clearly read about in the Bible.

But if there were anything inherent in the vicarious death concept I believe to be clearly taught in the Bible that demanded universalism or Calvinism, as some claim, then I would, no doubt, have some interest in the semantical gymnastics they go through to "prove" that it can't be true. But when one of these argues that a particular interpretation of a pertinent passage that appears to teach that Jesus died vicariously *can't* be interpreted that way because it has already been demonstrated that the doctrine isn't true, when he has, in fact, done no such thing, just makes me shake my head in disbelief that a brother in Christ would stoop to making such a statement—a statement that, ironically, is to be taken, *ipse dixit*, as an argument for *why* the doctrine isn't true.

Asking A Difficult Question

Those who take the above stated position are known to ask this supposed hard question: "To whom do you think the ransom price for our sins was paid?" If you say *to God*, which they wrongly think is the incorrect answer, they make reference to Anselm, the Archbishop of Canterbury, who, in the 11th century, was the first one to introduce the idea that the ransom or satisfaction was paid by Christ *not to Satan,* but to God. Then, we are quickly informed, the Reformers compounded Anselm's error by adding to it the idea that Jesus actually took the place of sinners in the sight of God and, as their substitute, suffered the punishment that was due them, including the sufferings of Hell. Upon Him, it is claimed these Reformers taught, fell all the punishment of all the sins of all the men for whom He died. Consequently, it was further argued that these Reformers believed that, because of Jesus' sacrifice, penal justice could have no further claim. As a result, the so-called

Substitution Theory was cross connected with the five points of Calvin, standing on the two legs of the imputation of our sins to Christ and the imputation of His righteousness to us.

To this I simply say, "So what!" What Anselm thought, or what the Reformers believed, is not really all that important to me, and I don't mean anything overtly disrespectful when I say this. What I believe about Jesus' vicarious death is based on what I can read in the Bible, not the philosophies and think-sos of men, be they Anselm, Luther, Calvin, Arminius, or even Thomas and Alexander Campbell. But what I can read in the Bible is very important to me, and I can read in the Bible much about Jesus' vicarious death.

"But That's Not Even In The Bible," They Argue

Someone retorts: "But *vicarious* isn't even in the Bible. Why then are you trying to defend it?" But, the fact that the actual word isn't used in the Scriptures doesn't mean the concept or idea is not taught there. For instance, where is the term "triune nature" found in the Bible? It isn't, but this does not mean that the idea isn't taught within its pages, and most Bible students acknowledge this. But to charge me, or anyone else, with bowing down to the dictates of the First Council of Nicaea because I believe in the triune nature of God is preposterous. Why, then, should brethren, who accuse me of believing and teaching something that is false because the word I'm using to identify it isn't found in the Bible, expect my opinion of them to remain intact when they resort to such tactics?

If I didn't have any other teaching but Isaiah 53, I would still believe Jesus was the divinely ordained sin-bearer. I would still believe that the iniquity of us all was, in fact, laid upon Him by the Father. I would still believe that He was wounded for our transgressions because God loved us that much. And finally, I would still believe that Jesus bore the sins of us all because God ordained it. However, when one adds to this the many passages that teach this very same idea, then I think I have every reason to believe in the vicarious death of Jesus, namely, that He died in my stead, paying the price that was owed for my sins, and not mine only, but for the sins of the whole world.[6]

This brings us full circle to this idea of Jesus being the "propitiation for our sins," and how it is in this truth that we are so confident of our salvation—not just now, but in the future, as well.

At Issue Is What The Bible, Not Calvinism, Teaches

As I've tried to demonstrate through this whole study of the errors of Calvinism, the main difference between Calvinism, a man-made doctrine, and the Bible, a divinely inspired revelation, is the idea that Calvinists believe that all the works of God in connection with our salvation are *unconditional*. Such thinking is required by their concept of God's sovereignty—a concept that by now should not surprise you to learn is not taught in the Bible. But when this erroneous concept is then joined with the equally erroneous idea that man, since the fall of Adam, is born totally depraved and is, therefore, not only *unwilling* to do God's will in such a state, but is actually *unable* to do so, then the false idea that God can't predestinate a person to be saved based on His foreknowledge of whether or not that person will meet certain divinely imposed *conditions* is the inevitable result. This, in turn, provides all the main ingredients that form the base of genuine five-point Calvinism (TULIP).

---

[6] 1 John 2:2.

In critiquing such an unscriptural idea, I have, at times, called it a "do-nothing religion,"[7] only to be met with screams and howls from Calvinists claiming this is a totally false caricature of their religion. However, if man does not have free will, and there are no genuine five-point Calvinists who have ever thought he does, and if, as has been amply pointed out, Calvinists believe that everything that has to do with man's salvation must be done by God, then Calvinism, from man's standpoint, may be properly classified as a do-nothing religion. Now, in saying this, I am not describing those who call themselves three- or four-point Calvinists, which are not really Calvinists at all, but Arminians. But, because the Augustinians/Calvinists have already decided that Arminianism is heresy, three- and four-pointers would never think of calling themselves Arminians. (Actually, the Calvinism vs. Arminianism dichotomy that exists in Christendom,[8] and the use the Calvinists have made of this, will be explored in the next chapter.)

So, there must be no doubt that five-point Calvinism, from man's standpoint, is a do-nothing religion, as God does it all, even to the point of selecting (viz., choosing/electing/predestinating) certain ones to obey His Son by operating upon them with His so-called "irresistible grace." This irresistible grace causes them to be born again, or renewed spiritually, so that they, in turn, are able to then do what it is that God requires of them. Consequently, there are absolutely no conditions to being saved, for if there were, Calvinists inform us, then man would be earning his salvation by works, not grace. Although this accurately depicts Calvinism, it does not describe New Testament Christianity at all.

---

7 See "Dialogue With A DO NOTHING Religionist," www.allanturner.com/dialogue8.html.

8 By using this term, I mean all the religious organizations and denominations that identify themselves as Christian.

What The Bible Actually Says

The Bible teaches that God decided to create us with free moral agency (for a more detailed discussion of this, refer to chapter 3). Because He has foreknowledge (see chapter 4), He knew His free will creatures were going to fall into sin and be in need of a Savior. Making the decision to redeem them, which was certainly not something He was obligated to do, He determined to send the *Logos* (or the divine Word) into this world as a man (viz., Jesus of Nazareth) to live and die so that mankind, in spite of its sinfulness, could be saved by faith in the only begotten Son of the Father.

Consequently, it was foreordained by God, the Father, before the very foundation of the world (i.e., before He created man) that Jesus would shed His blood at a particular time in the space-time continuum.[9] Referring to this, the apostle Paul said, "when the fullness of the time had come."[10]

The fact that God could foreknow, before He ever created them, that all His free will creatures would fall into sin and be in need of a Savior and that, in spite of this, He chose to go ahead and create them anyway, does not impugn the character of God, as some Christians seem to think. But why do they think so? Because, I think, they have inculcated Calvinistic think-sos and arguments. Now, I'm not saying they are Calvinists, mind you; only that they have been willing to let the Calvinists define the terms and set the parameters of the debate.

For example, and I pointed this out in chapters 2 and 3, the Calvinistic idea that there is somehow some sort of friction between God's foreknowledge and man's free will is not taught in the

---

9 See 1 Peter 1:19, 20.

10 Galatians 4:4.

Scriptures. But because some brethren have believed the Calvinists were right about this, then they have felt the necessity to defend man's free will by sacrificing God's foreknowledge. Such was a major error for the Calvinists and it is a major error for New Testament Christians, as well.

Even so, because of God's foreknowledge of the fact that man would sin *and* that this would, in turn, require Him to send His Son to pay the price for those sins, *and* that this would be accomplished by man *kissing* (viz., worshiping) His Son,[11] *and* that this would be achieved, on man's part, by exercising faith in Jesus as Lord *and*, ultimately, as Savior (stay with me here), He was able, in eternity, to do something—namely, to predestine not just the *plan* whereby He would redeem fallen man, *but exactly who those individuals were* who, when given the opportunity, would be willing, of their own free wills, to obey (or "kiss") His Son, doing so by rendering obedience to the gospel plan. (I know this is a very long sentence, but it is imperative to understanding this issue. So, if you didn't quite understand it the first or second time around, then please make the effort to do so before proceeding any further.)

Now, if God had not been willing to do this, and this even before the foundation of the world, then mankind was going to be lost. Therefore, if man is saved at all, he is saved by grace. But as we shall see, this salvation was not to be by grace alone. It was, and this is extremely important, to be by grace through faith. But for now, let's continue with the logical inferences and ramifications of the working in tandem of God's "determined counsel **and** foreknowledge."[12]

11 See Psalm 2:12 for this concept of kissing the Son and how the idea is tied to worshipful obedience.

12 Acts 2:23.

Thus, those individuals who God "chose...in Him [Jesus Christ] before the foundation of the world" were "predestined" by Him "to adoption as sons by Jesus Christ,...according to the good pleasure of His will."[13] That this was, even before creation, a *done deal* in the mind of God is once again confirmed and made quite clear by Romans 8:29, 30, which says:

> *For whom He foreknew, He also predestined to be conformed to the image of His Son, that He might be the firstborn among many brethren. Moreover whom He predestined, these He also called; whom He called, these He also justified; and whom He justified, these He also glorified.*

Furthermore, that the end result of this whole process is that these foreknown individuals (i.e., "the elect") would one day be glorified in Heaven cannot, according to this passage, be Scripturally denied, although I am sorry to say that I have known Christians who have tried to do so, arguing that the glorification mentioned here is only that which takes place on earth when an individual obeys the gospel. Now, I do not deny that our calling and justification is the *beginning* of this process, but glorification cannot be fully realized unless and until we obtain our glorified bodies. It is only then that we will fully and completely be conformed to the image of God's Son—a Son who is now glorified in heaven and, as such, is "the beginning, the firstborn from the dead,"[14] and all this that He might be able to bring "many sons to glory."[15]

That New Testament Christians could ever think of denying an idea that is so clearly taught in God's word demonstrates, once

---

13 Ephesians 1:4, 5.
14 Colossians 1:18.
15 Hebrews 2:10.

again, just how much Calvinistic thinking has influenced their thinking. Again, not that they are Calvinists, only that they are willing to deny (i.e., to explain away, if you will) the clear teaching of the Bible concerning the actual contents of God's foreknowledge, thinking that if God actually knew before the foundation of the world who it was that was going to be saved in Heaven, then the future would somehow be fixed in a way that would nullify man's free will.

However, the future is not "fixed" because God's foreknowledge has caused it to be that way. It is "fixed" only because this is the way free will creatures will respond to various circumstances and situations, and God, because HE IS WHO HE IS, simply foreknows what those contingent, free will choices will be. There is nothing inherently causative about such knowledge. (Again, I refer you back to chapters 3 and 4 for a more detailed discussion of this particular issue.)

But still suffering from the ol' Calvinistic bugaboo, someone says that if what I have written above is true, then this means that Jesus must have died just for the sins of the elect (that is to say, a limited few) and not for the sins of the whole world. But this simply isn't true. Although the elect were certainly foreknown by God even before He created the world, Jesus was not predestined to die *only* for the elect, as the Calvinists teach. No, no, no, a thousand times, no! Jesus, the Scriptures unequivocally teach, died for all mankind, not just a select few, and this, too, was a fact known by God before the foundation of the world.[16] (For a listing of these passages, please refer back to chapter 5, under the Limited Atonement subheading.)

---

16 1 Peter 1:20.

This means that before He actually created this particular world, God knew that only a few, relatively speaking, would be saved, and that the rest would be lost, spending an eternity, therefore, in a Devil's hell. Consequently, it is argued by some that if this is, in fact, the case (and it has been demonstrated that this is exactly what the Bible teaches), then how could a loving, merciful God think that the few who would be saved were worth the many who would be lost? This is an important point. Therefore, it behooves us to understand what we can about this perplexing subject.

Trying To Think It Through By Faith

As we try to think this out, even though we are limited by our puny, finite minds, we can theorize there must have been a multitude of different worlds that God, with His infinite knowledge (which included foreknowledge), could have created, all with a multitude of different outcomes. Why He chose this particular world, then, along with its particular results, is something completely known *only* by God. But, and this is now a foregone conclusion, He did decide to create this *particular* world with its *particular* outcome. Thus, before creating this world and knowing that many, many souls would be lost for an eternity as the result of His doing so, God did, in fact, choose to create this world: "In the beginning God created the heavens and the earth."[17]

It is just here, at the very first verse of the Bible, that saving faith begins, for faith, we are told in Romans 10:17 (and this is the saving faith we're talking about), "comes from hearing, and hearing by

---

[17] Genesis 1:1.

the word of God."[18] In Hebrews 11:3, after being informed in verse 1 that "faith is the substance of things hoped for, the evidence of things not seen," we are told: "By faith we understand that the worlds were framed by the word of God, so that the things which are seen were not made of things which are visible."

From this beginning verse—verse by verse, chapter by chapter, book by book—those of us who have been called by the glorious gospel of Jesus Christ[19] have learned to trust in and rely upon our Creator, who is, no doubt, our Ruler, but who is, as well, our glorious Redeemer, and praise God for it.

And it is just here, at the very beginning of saving faith, that we begin to get some idea why God determined that the remnant of His creation that would be saved and spend an eternity with Him in heaven was worth His creating this particular world. This will become more evident as we continue this study.

Thus, by the time we get to the pages of the New Testament, we are absolutely overjoyed to discover that the great scheme of redemption that was fully hidden in the mind of God before the foundation of the world has now been revealed to us, actualized in the fullness of time in the person of Jesus of Nazareth, who was Messiah (i.e., the Christ).[20] Oh, what magnificent grace and mercy! Oh, what wonderful, wonderful love!

The Calvinists are always arguing that if man is amenable to the gospel and is actually called upon to do anything in order to be saved, then salvation is by works instead of faith alone. However, as we've already learned, the Bible does not teach salvation by faith

---

18 Romans 10:17.

19 See 2 Thessalonians 2:14.

20 Consider what is said in Ephesians 3:5, coupled with the many other passages that tell us *who* Jesus was and *what* He came to accomplish.

alone. Nevertheless, it does teach that if man is going to be saved, it will have to be "by grace...through faith."[21] So, it is to this much misunderstood concept that we must now turn our attention.

Saved By Grace Through Faith

In chapter 8, we dealt with this subject in much greater detail. However, as it bears greatly on the security the Christian enjoys in connection with Christ, it is necessary that we go over it once again, but in much less detail than before.

Man does not have to sin; but he does. In fact, all have, or will, sin.[22] But the only way, under law, that a man can be saved is by perfect law-keeping, which no mere man has ever done. Therefore, if man is going to be saved, it will have to be because of God's grace. This grace, or unmerited favor, has been extended to us through His sending of His only begotten Son into this world to do what we had failed to do—namely, to perfectly keep, and thus fulfill, the law. Having done so, it could be set aside, or done away with, so that a new covenant, with better promises, could be instituted for man's salvation.[23]

So, it is theoretically possible for one to keep the law perfectly and go to Heaven. But because the rules under such a system require that *all* the law be kept *all* one's life, and because *all* mankind miserably failed in this, except Jesus of Nazareth, *all* mankind was in need of redemption. God was not obligated to redeem mankind, but He wanted to. Thus, He designed a plan (viz., the grand and

---

21 Ephesians 2:8.

22 See Romans 3:23.

23 See Hebrews 8:6; 12:24.

glorious Scheme of Redemption) whereby mankind could be redeemed.

Now, contrary to popular belief, God could not have saved man just any ol' way.[24] Redemption, if such was going to be implemented, would have to satisfy God's justice, and God's justice requires that any violation of law be punished. Jesus Christ, then, became the propitiation (or satisfaction) of such justice, which required that the only man who ever lived perfectly under law (thus qualifying as the spotless sacrifice, or propitiation, for the sins of all mankind) would pay the penalty for everyone else.[25] Thus, and as was pointed out in chapter 8, the only man who deserved glorification in Heaven, and this because He kept the law perfectly, suffered the penalty and, in so doing, became the propitiation for the sins of us all.

We must remember, then, that grace—and this is because it is grace—isn't *fair*. I know that sounds strange, but if you want fair, you must relate to God through a system of perfect law-keeping. Keep the law and you do not fall into condemnation; break the law and you become guilty of all, deserving the penalty that is due law-breaking. This is fair. But under such a system, all mankind, except for Jesus, sinned and, as a result, deserved the penalty. Nevertheless, because He loved us so much, God sent His only begotten Son into this world to effect our salvation through our willingness to accept His Son as our Lord and Savior. This brings us full circle, then. Why? Well, "If God is for us, who can be against us?"[26] And because God *is* for us, He did not spare His own Son, sacrificing Him for us:

---

24 See Romans 3:21-26.

25 2 Corinthians 5:14, 15.

26 Romans 8:31.

> *He who did not spare His own Son, but delivered Him up for us all, how shall He not with Him freely give us all things? Who shall bring a charge against God's elect? It is God who justifies. Who is he who condemns? It is Christ who died, and furthermore is also risen, who is even at the right hand of God, who also makes intercession for us.*[27]

It is clear, then, that God, in connection with His Son, has given us "all things." This means there is nothing lacking in connection with our redemption and continued salvation—not one single, solitary thing! Now, because God was able to justify us in connection with the sacrifice of His only begotten Son on the cross, who vicariously paid the price for our sins, no one can now bring a charge against His elect and make it stick. As has already been noted, this is absolutely fantastic. Thus, nothing is "able to separate us from the love of God which is in Christ Jesus our Lord."[28]

What all this means, once again, is that God is truly "for us," and in the next chapter, we'll look into this idea a bit further.

[27] Romans 8:32-34.
[28] Romans 8:39.

Chapter 12

What Does The Bible Mean When It Says That God Is "For Us"?

As has already been said, and as the above title suggests, the Bible teaches that God is, indeed, "for us." What does this really mean? In order to explore the answer to this question, we'll see that it involves the one and only true God being (1) our Friend, (2) our Helper, and (3) our Victory.

...*Our Friend*

As our Friend, God is on our side, willing and able to help us remain faithful to Him. As such, He has anticipated, and graciously supplied, our every spiritual need: "Blessed be the God and Father of our Lord Jesus Christ, who has blessed us with every spiritual blessing in the heavenly places in Christ."[1] This is precisely what the apostle Peter was writing about when he said:

> *Grace and peace be multiplied to you in the knowledge of God and of Jesus our Lord, as His divine power has given to us all things that pertain to life and godliness, through the knowledge of Him who called us by glory and virtue, by which have been given to us exceedingly great and precious promises, that through*

---

[1] Ephesians 1:3.

these you may be partakers of the divine nature, having escaped the corruption that is in the world through lust.[2]

As our Friend, God has graciously given us the Holy Spirit as a "deposit" of our salvation:

For all the promises of God in Him are Yes, and in Him Amen, to the glory of God through us. Now He who establishes us with you in Christ and has anointed us is God, who also has sealed us and given us the Spirit in our hearts as a deposit.[3]

In 2 Corinthians 5:1-6a, this deposit is called a "guarantee," and is clearly connected to the resurrected bodies we'll possess in our glorified state in the heavenly abode:

For we know that if our earthly house, this tent, is destroyed, we have a building from God, a house not made with hands, eternal in the heavens. For this we groan, earnestly desiring to be clothed with our habitation which is from heaven, if indeed, having been clothed, we shall not be found naked. For we who are in this tent groan, being burdened, not because we want to be unclothed, but further clothed, that mortality may be swallowed up by life. Now He who has prepared us for this very thing is God, who also has given us the Spirit as a guarantee. Therefore we are always confident....

Receiving this guarantee or deposit is referred to, in Ephesians 1:13-14, as being "sealed with the Holy Spirit of promise, who is the guarantee of our inheritance until the redemption of the purchased possession, to the praise of His glory."

---

[2] 2 Peter 1:2-4.

[3] 2 Corinthians 1:20, 22.

Clearly, then, God is the Friend who provides us with everything we need to become saved and, praise God, to stay saved. Therefore, with God on our side, as our Friend, we do not fear that, apart from our own wills, we can somehow lose our salvation.

This is verified again in John 10:28-29, which says:

And I give them eternal life and they shall never perish; neither shall anyone snatch them out of My hand. My Father who has given them to Me, is greater than all; and no one is able to snatch them out of My Father's hand.

And again in Colossians 1:2-6, where Paul says:

We give thanks to the God and Father of our Lord Jesus Christ, praying always for you, since we heard of your faith in Christ Jesus and of your love for all the saints; because of the hope which is laid up for you in heaven, of which you heard before in the word of the truth of the gospel, which has come to you, as it has also in the world, and is bringing forth fruit, as it is also among you since the day you heard and knew the grace of God in truth.

In other words, because God is our Friend, there is laid up for us a heavenly home, and it is in this hope that we are sustained, knowing that God is able to do for us exactly what He has promised He would do. Paul was referring to this very thing when, in 2 Timothy 4:8, he said, "Finally, there is laid up for me the crown of righteousness, which the Lord, the righteous Judge, will give to me on that Day, and not to me only but also to all who have loved His appearing."

Finally, the apostle Peter emphasized this same point when he wrote:

Blessed be the God and Father of our Lord Jesus Christ, who according to His abundant mercy has begotten us again to a living hope through the resurrection of Jesus Christ from the dead, to an inheritance incorruptible and undefiled and that does not fade away, reserved in heaven for you, who are kept by the power of God through faith for salvation ready to be revealed in the last time.[4]

...Our Helper

Not only is God our Friend, but He is our Helper as well. In this regard, it is helpful to view Jesus as our Elder Brother who is not ashamed to identify us as His brethren. This relationship is addressed in Hebrews 2:11-12, which says: "For both He who sanctifies and those who are being sanctified are all of one, for which reason He is not ashamed to call them brethren, saying: 'I will declare Your name to My brethren; in the midst of the congregation I will sing praise to You.'"[5] At the same time, Jesus, our Elder Brother, functions as our Mediator: "For there is one God and one Mediator between God and men, the Man Christ Jesus, who gave Himself a ransom for all."[6]

But this is not all, for the Scriptures inform us that He also serves as our Advocate. Addressing this, John wrote:

My little children, these things I write to you, that you may not sin. And if anyone sins, we have an Advocate with the Father, Jesus Christ the righteous.[7]

---

4 1 Peter 1:3-5.
5 This latter quote is taken from Psalm 22:22.
6 1 Timothy 2:5, 6a.
7 1 John 2:1.

In the very next verse, John links Jesus' advocacy on our behalf with the idea of propitiation, which is a concept that carries with it the idea of turning away God's wrath which, as sinners, we were unable to do for ourselves. In other words, not only did He give Himself for us, propitiating God's wrath, but having been resurrected from the dead, He now lives to make intercession for us on a regular basis.[8] As such, He is our merciful High Priest:

Therefore, in all things He had to be made like His brethren, that He might be a merciful High Priest in things pertaining to God, to make propitiation for the sins of the people. For in that He Himself has suffered, being tempted, He is able to aid those who are tempted.[9]

Consequently, it is not just that God, through Christ's blood, has saved us from our past sins, but He continues to do so through that same blood:

But if we walk in the light as He is in the light, we have fellowship with one another, and the blood of Jesus Christ His Son cleanses us from all sin. If we say we have no sin, we deceive ourselves, and the truth is not in us. If we confess our sins, He is faithful and just to forgive us our sins and to cleanse us from all unrighteousness.[10]

As our Helper, the Lord delivers us from temptation. This is made clear in 1 Corinthians 10:13, which says:

No temptation has overtaken you except such as is common to man; but God is faithful, who will not allow you to be tempted

8 See Hebrews 7:25.
9 Hebrews 2:17, 18.
10 1 John 1:7-9.

beyond what you are able, but with the temptation will also make the way of escape, that you may be able to bear it.

And as if this is not enough, as our Helper, the Holy Spirit, we are told in Romans 8:26, makes intercession for us:

Likewise the Spirit also helps in our weaknesses. For we do not know what we should pray for as we ought, but the Spirit Himself makes intercession for us with groanings which cannot be uttered.

Even angels, according to Hebrews 1:14, come to our assistance:

Are they not all ministering spirits sent forth to minister for those who will inherit salvation?

Again, in Hebrews 12:22, it is said:

But you have come to Mount Zion and the city of the living God, the heavenly Jerusalem, to an innumerable company of angels.

Furthermore, we are assured in Ephesians 3:16 that God, as our faithful and dependable Helper, strengthens us in the "inner man." This is further amplified in Philippians 4:13, which says, "I can do all things through Christ who strengthens me." Such wonderful and exhilarating help caused David, in Psalm 28:6, 7, to exult:

Blessed be the Lord, because He has heard the voice of my supplications! The Lord is my strength and my shield; my heart trusted in Him, and I am helped; therefore my heart greatly rejoices, and with my song I will praise Him.

Finally, as our caring Helper, God sometimes even chastens us for our own good, as Hebrews 12:5-7 points out:

And you have forgotten the exhortation which speaks to you as to sons: "My son, do not despise the chastening of the LORD, nor be discouraged when you are rebuked by Him; for whom the LORD loves He chastens, and scourges every son whom He receives." If you endure chastening, God deals with you as with sons; for what son is there whom a father does not chasten?

Then, there are those blessings our Helper has designed specifically for us in order to aid in the security of believers. The first of these is the Congregation Relationship and is mentioned in Hebrews 10:24-25:

And let us consider one another in order to stir up love and good works, not forsaking the assembling of ourselves together, as is the manner of some, but exhorting one another, and so much the more as you see the Day approaching.

The Lord knew that we needed each other, and all of us who have had the privilege of associating with other Christians know full-well the encouraging advantage of our fellow saints.

Next, we'll look at the Special Servants our glorious Helper has blessed us with. This is seen from a reading of Ephesians 4:11-16, which says:

And He Himself gave some to be apostles, some prophets, some evangelists, and some pastors and teachers, for the equipping of the saints for the work of ministry, for the edifying of the body of Christ, till we all come to the unity of the faith and of the knowledge of the Son of God, to a perfect man, to the measure of the stature of the fullness of Christ; that we should no longer be children, tossed to and fro and carried about with every wind of doctrine, by the trickery of men, in the cunning craftiness of deceitful plotting, but, speaking the truth in love, may grow up in all things into Him who is the head -- Christ -- from whom the whole body, joined and knit together by what every joint supplies, according to the effective working by which every part does its share, causes growth of the body for the edifying of itself in love.

Then there is the actual Lord's Day and the assembling associated with it:

Now on the first day of the week, when the disciples came together to break bread, Paul ready to depart the next day, spoke to them and continued his message until midnight.[11]

Let the word of Christ dwell in you richly in all wisdom, teaching and admonishing one another in psalms and hymns and spiritual songs, singing with grace in your hearts to the Lord.[12]

In connection with this, of course, is...

The Lord's Supper:

For I received from the Lord that which I also delivered to you: that the Lord Jesus on the same night in which He was betrayed took bread; and when He had given thanks, He broke it and said, "Take, eat; this is My body which is broken for you; do this in remembrance of Me." In the same manner He also took the cup after supper, saying, "This cup is the new covenant in My blood. This do, as often as you drink it, in remembrance of Me." For as often as you eat this bread and drink this cup, you proclaim the Lord's death till He comes.[13]

---

11 Acts 20:7.
12 Colossians 3:16.
13 1 Corinthians 11:23-26.

The Scriptures:

> *All Scripture is given by inspiration of God, and is profitable for doctrine, for reproof, for correction, for instruction in righteousness, that the man of God may be complete, thoroughly equipped for every good work.*[14]

And Prayer:

> *Be anxious for nothing, but in everything by prayer and supplication, with thanksgiving, let your requests be made known to God; and the peace of God, which surpasses all understanding, will guard your hearts and minds through Christ Jesus.*[15]

...Our Victory

As our Victory, God defeats Satan for us. As a result, we can be sure that the Lord fights our battles for us:

> *And Asa cried out to the Lord his God, and said, "Lord it is nothing for You to help, whether with many or with those who have no power; help us, O Lord, You are our God..."*[16]

> *"Be strong and courageous, do not be afraid nor dismayed before the king of Assyria, nor before all the multitude that is with him; for there are more with us than with him. With him is an arm of flesh; but with us is the Lord our God, to help us and to fight our*

---

[14] 2 Timothy 3:16, 17.
[15] Philippians 4:6, 7.
[16] 2 Chronicles 14:11.

> *battles." And the people were strengthened by the words of Hezekiah king of Judah.*[17]

> *And when the servant of the man of God arose early and went out, there was an army, surrounding the city with horses and chariots. And his servant said to him, "Alas, my master! What shall we do?" So he answered, "Do not fear, for those who are with us are more than those who are with them." And Elisha prayed, and said, "Lord, I pray, open his eyes that he may see." Then the Lord opened the eyes of the young man, and he saw. And behold, the mountain was full of horses and chariots of fire all around Elisha.*[18]

Consequently, the Christian's faith is in God's power, not our own abilities, and this is exactly what Paul taught when he wrote that our faith "should not be in the wisdom of men but in the power of God."[19] Elsewhere he explained that it was his desire that all Christians be able to fathom just "what is the exceeding greatness of His power toward us who believe, according to the working of His mighty power."[20]

This means that with God as our Victory, overcoming evil is something we can be quite confident of because, "You are of God, little children, and have overcome them, because He who is in you is greater than He who is in the world."[21] This is, indeed, reminiscent of what Elisha told his servant in 2 Kings 6:16.

Therefore, whatever confidence and boldness the Christian has are possible because of God's magnificent triumphs, particularly in

---

17 2 Chronicles 32:7, 8.
18 2 Kings 6:15-17.
19 1 Corinthians 2:5.
20 Ephesians 1:19.
21 1 John 4:4.

His grand Scheme of Redemption: "[A]ccording to the eternal purpose which He accomplished in Christ Jesus our Lord, in whom we have boldness and access with confidence through faith in Him."[22] This is explained further in the following passages:

> *For if our heart condemns us, God is greater than our hearts, and knows all things. Beloved, if our heart does not condemn us, we have confidence toward God. And whatever we ask we receive from Him, because we keep His commandments, and do those things that are pleasing in His sight.*[23]

> *Love has been perfected among us in this: that we may have boldness in the day of judgment; because as He is, so are we in this world. There is no fear in love; but perfect love casts out fear, because fear involves torment. But he who fears has not been made perfect in love.*[24]

> *Seeing then that we have a great High Priest who has passed through the heavens, Jesus the Son of God, let us hold fast our confession. For we do not have a High Priest who cannot sympathize with our weaknesses, but was in all points tempted as we are, yet without sin. Let us therefore come boldly to the throne of grace, that we may obtain mercy and find grace to help in time of need.*[25]

And finally, in Philippians 4:6-7:

> *Be anxious for nothing, but in everything by prayer and supplication, with thanksgiving, let your requests be known to God;*

---

22 Ephesians 3:11, 12.
23 1 John 3:20-22.
24 1 John 4:17, 18.
25 1 John 4:14-16.

and the peace of God, which surpasses all understanding, will guard your hearts and minds through Christ Jesus.

In summary, there can be no doubt in the believer's mind that God is for us! As our Friend, He is on our side, willing and able to help us remain faithful. As our Helper, He protects us and provides for our spiritual welfare. As our Victory, He defeats Satan for us. Consequently, along with Paul, we glorify our great Friend, wonderful Helper, and our absolute Victory by exclaiming:

Now to Him who is able to do exceedingly abundantly above all that we ask or think, according to the power that works in us, to Him be glory in the church by Christ Jesus throughout all ages, world without end. Amen.[26]

---

[26] Ephesians 3:20, 21.

Chapter 13

The Great Calvinism Versus Arminianism Hoodwink

Back when I was in my mid-twenties, I encountered an inquisitive bookstore owner who asked me about my religious "affiliation." "What are you, religiously?," he asked. My "I'm a Christian" reply was less than satisfactory, for he said, "Of course, aren't we all?" When I responded by saying I didn't think so, he got his dander up a bit. I'd been in his bookstore a few times and he was evidently having a problem identifying my particular brand of "Christianity." He had made up his mind that he just didn't want to know *who* I was, but wanted to know *what* I was, as well. "Where do you go to church?," he asked. When I told him, he asked, "Are y'all Calvinists or Arminians?" "Neither," I responded. "Well, you've got to be one or the other," he said, "so let me ask you this: Do you believe a child of God can fall from grace?" "Yes, I do," I replied. "Well, you're an Arminian, then!" "No, I'm not," I said. "Yes, you are," he insisted. "No, I'm not!," I emphasized.

Well, I could go on, but I think you catch my drift here: Many people, particularly Calvinists, believe Christendom is divided into two camps: one Calvinist, the other Arminian—the first, the orthodox position, the second, the heretical one. How did this come to be the thinking of so many? The answer is interesting and explains why so many think Calvinism to be the one true brand of Christianity.

Arminianism

Jacobus (James) Arminius was a Dutch theologian who lived from 1560-1609. While attending the Geneva Academy, which was Calvin's seminary, he was a student of Theodore Beza, who was not just Calvin's son-in-law, but his hand-picked successor. Before studying with Beza, he had already been exposed to various teachings that caused him to question the Calvinistic idea that ever since Adam's sin all mankind was guilty of Adam's sin and, therefore, totally depraved (Augustine's idea of Original Sin). Instead, Arminius came to believe that one incurs guilt only when he chooses (voluntarily) to sin.

Although it is fairly safe to say that Arminius started out a strict Calvinist, there can be no doubt that he later modified his views considerably. Arminius never formerly systematized his views. However, a year after his death, in 1610, his convictions were assembled by his disciples and presented in a document called *The Remonstrance.* Arminianism, as it came to be known, became the theological foundation for the Methodist, Wesleyan, Nazarene, Pentecostal, Free Will Baptist, Holiness, and many charismatic churches. Like Calvinism, it is articulated by five basic tenets:

> 1. **Election based on knowledge**, the belief that God chose those who would be saved in eternity past based on His foreknowledge of those who would respond to and receive the Gospel of Jesus Christ. Arminianism rejects the concept that God elected anyone for hell.
>
> 2. **Unlimited atonement** is the belief that Jesus died on the Cross for all people, that His blood is sufficient to pay the penalty for the sins of every man, woman, and child who has ever lived. Thus, all mankind is salvable.

3. **Natural inability** is the teaching that man cannot save Himself, but that the Holy Spirit must effect the new birth in him. Strict Arminians do not believe that man is totally depraved and condemned as a result of Adam's sin.

4. **Prevenient grace** is the Arminian belief that the prepatory work of the Holy Spirit enables the believer to respond to the Gospel and to cooperate with God in the working out of that person's salvation.

5. **Conditional perseverance** is the belief that man can choose to reject God, and therefore lose his salvation, even after he has been born again. Rather than the "once saved always saved" doctrine of the Calvinists, the Arminian believes that you must abide in Christ to be saved, and that you can choose to walk away from God. Arminius himself, and his early followers, stated that they were not really sure of this doctrine and that it required further study of God's word. Later, however, Arminians are reported to have accepted it.

Neither A Catholic, Protestant, Calvinist, Nor Arminian Be

As you've already learned from this study, I am not a Calvinist, although my view on God's absolute foreknowledge has caused me to be wrongly accused of being one by some of my brethren. Even so, and this will, no doubt, be difficult for both Calvinists and Arminians to comprehend (especially Calvinists), I make no claim of being an Arminian either. Yes, I do believe Arminius was closer to being right than were the Calvinists, but there are things he clearly did not get right either. For example, Arminius believed humans to be naturally unable to make any effort towards salvation. Those who followed in his footsteps called this "Prevenient grace." Such was described in Article VIII of the *Articles of Religion*, which John Wesley adapted for use by American Methodists:

> *The condition of man after the fall of Adam is such that he cannot turn and prepare himself, by his own natural strength and works, to faith, and calling upon God; wherefore we have no power to do good works, pleasant and acceptable to God, without the grace of God by Christ preventing [preceding] us, that we may have a good will, and working with us, when we have that good will.*

The Bible, of course, teaches no such thing and this kind of thinking is nothing but a denial of the free moral agency (viz., free will) of man. Thus, it is clear to me that Arminius and his followers believed and taught things that are contrary to God's word. Like the Protestants before them, they accepted some of the theological ideas that were then prevalent, instead of deriving their thinking from the Bible *alone*.

For example, although the popular Protestant slogan had been *sola Scriptura*, or "the Scriptures only," Luther's primary motivation was to simply reform, not restore, "the church." Of course, he should have actually gone back to the Bible as the sole authority for what he believed and practiced, instead of just giving lip service to it, as he did.

Unfortunately, one encounters the same from contemporary reformers, regardless of their denominational affiliations, who, instead of citing the Bible as their source of authority, want to talk about the way the so-called "church fathers" viewed a particular practice or doctrine, arguing that man-made think-sos establish the patterns that can safely be followed by contemporary "Christians."

Likewise, Arminius and his followers, instead of rejecting some, or even most, of Calvin's think-sos, should have returned to the Bible *alone* for what they believed and practiced.

Why The Calvinism Versus Arminianism Dichotomy?

Nevertheless, Calvinists have decided that a Calvinism-Arminianism division affords strength to their theological system, in that it helps foster the idea that Calvinism, which all good Calvinists argue is the true teaching of Christianity, is only opposed by one monolithic, heretical, anti-Biblical system—namely, Arminianism. In other words, if you're not a Calvinist, you're an Arminian; and if you're an Arminian, you're a heretic, is the charge the Calvinists try to make stick. As Boettner puts it:

> *It must be evident that there are just two theories which can be maintained by evangelical Christians upon this important subject; that all men who have made any study of it, and who have reached any settled conclusions regarding it, must be either Calvinists or Arminians. There is no other position which a "Christian" can take.*[1]

And as the "Rev." C. Matthew McMahon, Ph.D., wrote on his website, *A Puritan's Mind*:

> *The system of doctrine known as Arminianism is heresy. It is an offshoot from Pelagianism and Semi-Pelagianism. It has been adversely affecting the church and its doctrine for over 250 years. Men like Finney and Wesley, being the charismatic personalities they were, propagated the doctrine and resurrected the*

---

[1] Loraine Boettner, *The Reformed Doctrine of Predestination*, 1932, page 333.

Pelagian error from the pit of hell once again to persecute the church of Christ. (In an article entitled, "Arminianism: The heresy plaguing the modern church of the 21st century. What is it and where did it come from?"*).*[2]

So, it is evident that Calvinists like to identify their man-made theology as being true orthodoxy, while branding everything else as Arminianism and, therefore, absolute and total heresy. This, they think, makes their job of holding their followers in check a whole lot easier.

The Synod Of Dort And The Old Charge Of Pelagianism

They got off to a good start with the now famous (infamous, depending how you look at it) Synod of Dort, which was convened in the Dutch city of Dordrecht by the Dutch Reformed Church on November 13, 1618. During this national assembly that lasted until May 9, 1619 (which was also attended by voting representatives from eight other countries), and in direct response to Arminianism's rejection of unconditional election, as articulated by Calvin and his followers, it was affirmed that:

This election [namely, unconditional election] was not founded upon foreseen faith, and the obedience of faith, holiness, or any other good quality or disposition in man, as the prerequisite, cause, or condition on which it depended; but men are chosen to the obedience of faith, holiness, etc. Therefore, election is the fountain of every saving good; from which proceed faith, holiness, and the other gifts of salvation, and finally eternal life itself, as fruits and effects, according to that of the apostle: "He hath

---

2 www.apuritansmind.com/Arminianism/Arminianism.htm.

chosen us (not because we were [or would be], but) that we should be holy, and without blame, before him in love." Ephesians 1:4.[3]

Notice, if you will (and this is very important), that the synod proclaimed that faith is the *fruit* and *effect* of predestination, not its *condition* or *prerequisite*, as the Arminian position is alleged to have argued. Citing Ephesians 1:4, they claimed that God chose the elect *in order to give* them (not *because of* their) faith, repentance, *et cetera*. That this is consistent with what Calvin had taught is clear by observing that in his comments on Ephesians 1:4, he wrote:

Besides, the fact that they were elected "to be holy" plainly refutes the error that derives election from foreknowledge, since Paul declares all virtue appearing in man is the result of election.... [S]ay: "since he foresaw that we would be holy, he chose us," and you will invert Paul's order. Therefore you can safely infer the following: if he chose us that we should be holy, he did not choose us because he foresaw that we would be so."

But evidently hoping to nail the Arminian coffin shut once and for all, the Synod of Dort identified Arminians as purveyors of Pelagianism and Semi-Pelagianism, a "heresy" that had been "dealt with" more than a thousand years earlier by the Council of Ephesus (also known as the Third Ecumenical Council) in A.D. 431. But even before this, in A.D. 417, Pelagius (who we know very little about) had already been excommunicated by Pope Innocent I for teaching that, since Adam's fall, man is not born totally depraved and, thus, of his own free will can decide to obey God or not. Pelagius, who was no doubt wrong on some things and right

---

[3] First Head, Article 9, Divine Election And Reprobation.

on others, got into trouble because his teaching on free moral agency contradicted Augustine of Hippo's (A.D. 354-430) teaching on Original Sin—a position that became the official position of the Roman Catholic Church. In fact, B.B. Warfield has identified Augustine as being "in a true sense the founder of Roman Catholicism."[4] So, when Pelagius contradicted Augustine, it was a foregone conclusion that he would quickly be branded a troublesome heretic.

Consequently, and don't miss the irony here, when the Dutch Reformed Church, a Protestant denomination, labeled Arminians as being infected with Pelagianism, they were validating the findings of a religious organization they were supposed to be officially protesting. Furthermore, that Augustine was adored, even revered, by Calvin, who called him a "holy man" and "holy father,"[5] remains one of the strange ironies of Reformed Theology and demonstrates, conclusively, that the Reformers were not willing to jettison the theological encumbrances of an apostate "Mother Church" for the truths taught in God's word, even while they argued their "Sola Scriptura" slogan.

"Mongrels," "Middle-Grounders" And The So-Called "Three-Sided Coin"

Thus, the either/or dichotomies (viz., Catholicism or Protestantism; Calvinism or Arminianism) serve to denominate, simplify, and degrade the precious truths taught in God's word with the competing theologies of man-made philosophies and ideas. Specifically, the dichotomies mentioned taint the whole of

[4] *Calvin and Augustine*, 1956, page 313.

[5] Laurence M. Vance, *The Other Side Of Calvinism*, 1999, pages 139, 146, 148, 149.

modern Christendom, and so much so that anyone who makes the claim of being *neither* a Calvinist *nor* an Arminian is identified as some sort of a doctrinal "mongrel" or "middle-grounder" who is wrongly claiming a third side to what "everyone knows" is only a two-sided theological coin.[6]

It is exactly this kind of thinking that I'm calling the Calvinist Hoodwink—a devious, diabolical deception that favors Augustinianism/Calvinism, or whatever one might want to call the determinism that pervades Catholicism and saturates Protestantism, over and against something called Arminianism, which has become the catch-all moniker that determinists use to describe and identify any concept that differs from their own.

A Few Examples

For example, Norman L. Geisler, a prolific writer (he has authored and coauthored over sixty books) and President of Southern Evangelical Seminary in Charlotte, North Carolina, likes to call himself a "moderate" Calvinist, as opposed to an "extreme" or "hyper" Calvinist (these are all his terms—*AT*). When you listen to his views, which he outlines extensively in *Chosen To Be Free: A Balanced View Of Divine Election*, he sounds much like an Arminian. But to actually admit to Arminianism, he must know, would clearly place him in the heretic's camp, so he revels in and extols what he calls "moderate Calvinism"—the kind of Calvinism he believes embodies true Christianity.

[6] For an example of this, consider Jim Bublitz's Internet blog at www.oldtruth.com/blog.cfm/id.2.pid.286.

Nevertheless, some of his fellow Calvinists have berated him for actually being an Arminian masquerading in Calvinistic garb.[7] In other words, and true to the smoke and mirror effects of the Calvinist Hoodwink, one will, theologically speaking, either dot his theological *i*'s and cross his theological *t*'s the way "true" Calvinists do, or he will be labeled an Arminian, which is just another way of calling him a rank heretic, who must then be identified and avoided.

For example, in a review of James White's book, which is referred to in the footnote at the bottom of this page, Jay Adams, Ph.D., of Westminster Seminary in Escondido, California, wrote:

> The Potter's Freedom *is a more than adequate response to the misleading and erroneous book,* Chosen but Free, *by Norman Geisler. Indeed, it is a fresh and helpful statement of true Calvinism over against a system purporting to be "Calvinistic" which is really nothing more than a brand of Arminianism. This book should be widely disseminated and read as it will clarify much that is often misunderstood about Calvinism.*[8]

The Bible Teaches Neither Calvinism Nor Arminianism

But the Calvinist Hoodwink notwithstanding, the Bible, in reality, teaches neither Calvinism nor Arminianism. Both are theological constructs that honor man's thinking and not the teachings found in the Bible. This, in spite of the fact that Reformed Theol-

---

7 See James R. White, *The Potter's Freedom,* 2000.

8 At www.aomin.org/TPF.html, the website of Alpha & Omega Ministries.

ogy, as it is called by Calvinists, is claimed by them to be "firmly based...upon the Word of God."[9]

As my friends know, I come from a part of the South where "everyone's a Baptist unless someone's been 'messing' with him," as we southerners are wont to say. Consequently, I have been confronted by many of my Baptist friends and relatives with the tenets of Calvinism, which they believed to be the essence of the gospel of Jesus Christ. As some of them insisted, "If you do not know the Five Points of Calvinism, you do not know the gospel, but some perversion of it..."[10] At the same time, more than a few of my Baptist neighbors argued for something slightly different than the theological demands of Five Point Calvinism.

For example, many of them, although they might readily admit to being Calvinists, had abandoned the idea that children were born totally depraved. They also rejected the idea that unregenerated man was unable to exercise faith in the gospel of Christ. In fact, exercising faith was something (actually, practically the *only* something) that was *required* of man in order to be saved. So, it was clear to me that there was a very broad spectrum of thinking among my Baptist neighbors on whether or not man was so depraved that he was totally unable to respond by faith to the gospel of Jesus Christ.

But not being a Baptist, I had no idea of the extent of the debate that was taking place among them over the tenets of Five Point Calvinism. I frequently thought that Baptists, who I believed to be Calvinistic doctrinally, were either ignorant of Calvinism's tenets or had simply rebelled at some of its teachings because they

[9] Jimmie B. Davis, *The Berea Baptist Banner*, February 5, 1995, page 30.

[10] Fred Phelps, "The Five Points of Calvinism," *The Berea Baptist Banner*, February 5, 1990, page 21.

thought them much too harsh. Little did I realize that those associated with the Southern Baptist Convention, the ones that represented the majority of the Baptists I knew, do not actually consider themselves Five Point Calvinists. There are, of course, a multitude of different kinds of Baptists, but although there is reported to have been a resurgence of Five Point Calvinism in the ranks of Southern Baptists, many of them (I'm talking about their "pastors") are, in fact, woefully inconsistent, rarely employing their theology lest their evangelistic and missionary endeavors suffer.[11] As Dave Hunt has noted in a book critiquing Calvinism:

> *If grace truly is irresistible, if only those elected by God to salvation can be saved, if no one can believe the gospel until regenerated by God and thereafter given the faith to believe, would it not be vain to attempt to persuade anyone through the gospel—or for those who hear to attempt to believe in Christ? Since there is nothing one can do to change one's eternal destiny (if one of the elect, nothing can stand between the soul and heaven; and if not among the elect, nothing can be done to escape hell) shouldn't one just go on with life and let the inevitable take its course? While many Calvinists would object to this view, it cannot be denied that this is the practical conclusion to which that dogma leads.*[12]

Satan surely must smile at the cognitive dissonance that must reign within the confines of Reformed Theology, for if Calvinism is right, then all the money and effort spent on evangelism and missionary work appears to be redundant or "Much Ado About Nothing," as William Shakespeare would have dubbed it.

---

11 Vance, *op. cit.*, page 25.

12 *What Love Is This?*, 2002, page 352.

No Three- Or Two-Sided Coins

When it comes to Bible doctrine, there are, for sure, no three-sided coins; but there are no two-sided coins either. In 1 Corinthians 1:10-11, the apostle Paul said:

> *Now I plead with you, brethren, by the name of our Lord Jesus Christ, that there be no divisions among you, but that you all be perfectly joined together in the same mind and in the same judgment. For it has been declared to me concerning you, my brethren, by those of Chloe's household, that there are contentions among you.*

Paul makes it clear that Christianity is not three- or even two-sided. Instead, it is simply one-sided, and he drove this point home in verses 12 and 13 by saying:

> *Now I say this, that each of you says, "I am of Paul," or "I am of Apollos," or "I am of Cephas," or "I am of Christ." Is Christ divided? Was Paul crucified for you? Or were you baptized in the name of Paul?*

Then in 1 Corinthians 3:2-4, he concludes:

> *[F]or you are still carnal. For where there are envy, strife, and divisions among you, are you not carnal and behaving like mere men? For when one says, "I am of Paul," and another, "I am of Apollos," are you not carnal?*

Is it not appropriate, then, to admonish the adherents of Calvin and Arminius with, "For when one says, 'I am of Calvin,' and another, 'I am of Arminius,' are you not carnal?"

The Broad Way And The Narrow Way

Yes, it is true that this thing called Christendom is not just two- or three-sided. It is, in essence, many-sided, for there are, in fact, hundreds, even thousands, of churches today that claim to be following the Christ. Of these, some claim to be Catholic, others Protestant, some Augustinian/Calvinist, others Arminian, *et cetera, et cetera*. It is my contention, and I believe the clear teaching of Scripture, that none of this—not one single, solitary bit of it—honors Him who was crucified for *all* of us.[13] It is not the "narrow way" so clearly and painstakingly set forth in God's word,[14] nor does it represent the "faith which was once for all delivered to the saints."[15] Thus, in what remains of this chapter, permit me to state, as succinctly as I know how, that very narrow way we can read about in the pages of the New Testament.

The "My Church" Of Matthew 16:18

In Matthew 16:18, Jesus said, "I will build My church." So, it is the "My church" of this passage, and not some religious denomination, that I want to talk to you about. But in order to do this, you must be willing to set aside all religious prejudice and denominational bias and simply consider the truths taught in God's Word on this most important subject.

In Ephesians 4:4, the Bible teaches there is but one body. In Colossians 1:18, we learn this "one body" is none other than the church belonging to Christ. In other words, the "My church" of

---

13 See 2 Corinthains 5:14, 15; 2 Timothy 3, 4.

14 See Matthew 7:13, 14 and 1 Corinthains 2:12, 13.

15 Jude 3.

Matthew 16:18 is the body, or church, of Christ.[16] As such, Christ is the church's only Head. This means that no man, be he the Pope of Rome, or any other, is the head of Christ's church.

In Ephesians 2:16, the Bible teaches that all mankind, whether Jew or Gentile, are reconciled in the one body "by the cross" (cf. v. 13). Consequently, it ought not to surprise us that the church was purchased by Jesus' blood on the cross, and this is exactly what the Bible says in Acts 20:28. Therefore, those who are identified as being in the body are also described as being blood-bought.[17] To be in Christ, then, is to be in His body, and to be in His body is to be in His church. If this is true, and the Bible clearly teaches us that it is, then a significant question would be: *"How does one get into the church—or body—of Christ?"*

The Lord Adds To His Church Those Who Obey Him

In Acts 2:47, we learn that "the Lord added to the church daily those who were being saved." This is certainly as it should be, because Christ is the "author of eternal salvation unto all them that obey Him."[18] In order to be saved and added to the Lord's church, one must be willing to obey Him. In 1 Samuel 15:22, Samuel, guided by the Holy Spirit, informed Saul that "to obey is better than sacrifice." The apostle John, inspired by the same Spirit that inspired Samuel, wrote, "He who says, 'I know Him,' and does not keep His commandments, is a liar, and the truth is not in Him."[19]

---

16 See Ephesians 1:22.

17 See 1 Corinthians 6:20; 1 Peter 1:18, 19.

18 Hebrews 5:9.

19 1 John 2:4.

Obedience Is Absolutely Necessary

The Lord said, "...if you do not believe that I am He, you will die in your sins."[20] In Acts 17:30, the apostle Paul said, "Truly, these times of ignorance God overlooked, but now commands all men everywhere to repent." In Romans 10:10, we are taught that in order to be saved one must be willing to confess Jesus Christ.[21] While many are willing to acknowledge the importance of *belief*, *repentance*, and *confession* of Jesus as Lord in relationship to salvation by grace, they reject the idea that baptism has anything at all to do with salvation. This, of course, is terribly unfortunate, because the Bible unequivocally teaches that baptism, like belief, repentance and confession, is absolutely necessary in order to be saved. If, for whatever reason, you doubt this, then I challenge you to invest the time to seriously contemplate the Scriptures we are about to consider.

Baptized Into Christ

In Galatians 3:27, Paul makes it quite clear that we are "baptized into Christ." In other words, we are "baptized into one body."[22] Unquestionably, then, one cannot be "in Christ" (i.e., in a saved relationship with Him) unless one has been baptized. This is why baptism, in Acts 2:38, is said to be "for [i.e., unto, or for the purpose of] the remission of sins." This is why Saul of Tarsus was told: "And now why are you waiting? Arise and be baptized, and wash

---

[20] John 8:24.

[21] See also Matthew 10:32, 33.

[22] 1 Corinthians 12:13.

away your sins, calling on the name of the Lord."[23] This is why the apostle Peter said, "...baptism doth now also save us" in 1 Peter 3:21 (KJV). And this is why the Colossian letter refers to baptism as the "circumcision of Christ."[24] Under the Law of Moses, circumcision, the cutting away of the flesh, was a sign of being in covenant relationship with God. Consequently, the circumcision of Christ, the cutting off or putting away of the sins of the flesh, is a sign of being in covenant relationship with God through Jesus Christ. If you have not been baptized to "wash away your sins," then you are not in a covenant relationship with Christ.

Religious people have many erroneous ideas about baptism. Some think that Holy Spirit baptism was promised to every believer. It wasn't. The baptism of the Holy Spirit was a gift to be received, not a commandment to be obeyed, and the only two occasions of it being given are to the apostles in Acts 1:26-2:13 and Cornelius' household in Acts 10:44-46 and 11:11. But different from these events, we hear the Bible speaking of "one baptism"[25] which, according to Acts 10:47 and 8:36, has to be water baptism. Thus, we can be sure that the baptism commanded in Acts 2:38 was water baptism.

Furthermore, some think the mode of baptism can be sprinkling, pouring, or immersion. However, the Greek word for "baptized" is *baptizo*, and it means, according to *Strong's Greek Lexicon*, "to dip, to immerse, to submerge." This is why the Bible, in several places, refers to baptism as a burial.[26] Therefore, an individual who has been sprinkled or poured has not been scripturally baptized.

---

[23] Acts 22:16.

[24] Colossians 2:11, 12.

[25] Ephesians 4:5.

[26] See Colossians 2:12; Romans 6:4.

This will be shocking to some of you who read this, but please remember that I am endeavoring to "speak as the oracles [or word] of God,"[27] not the think-sos of men.

So, although it is true that certain churches, reflecting the doctrines of men, sprinkle and pour their members, calling either of these modes *baptism*, the Bible, as we've already seen, says that baptism is a burial or immersion in water. Therefore, the Bible teaches there is one, and only one, Scriptural mode of baptism. This means that if you haven't been immersed, then you haven't been Scripturally baptized.

In addition, some religious organizations, particularly the Roman Catholic Church, teach that infants are proper subjects of baptism. However, the New Testament nowhere speaks of infant baptism. The only people the Bible mentions who are the proper subjects of baptism are those who *hear the gospel*,[28] *repent of their sins*,[29] and *confess Jesus as Lord*.[30] Clearly, then, infants are unable to do this, as they simply do not have the moral capacity to do so. Consequently, infants can't be the proper subjects of baptism. Besides, baptism is "for the remission of sins,"[31] and infants do not have any sins that need to be remitted. The concept that infants are born totally depraved or with the taint of original sin is a tenet of Augustinianism or Calvinism, not the Bible. The Bible, in point of fact, says nothing about this man-made doctrine—nothing at all.

---

27 1 Peter 4:11.
28 See Romans 10:17.
29 See Acts 17:30.
30 See Romans 10:10; Acts 8:37b.
31 Acts 2:38.

There Is A Relationship Between Jesus' Blood And Baptism

Those who believe that baptism is not necessary for the remission of sins frequently teach that an emphasis on baptism diminishes the blood of Christ, making it of no effect. Such teaching could not be further from the truth.

The Bible teaches there is, in fact, a relationship between the blood of Christ and baptism.[32] In Matthew 26:28, we learn that Jesus' blood was shed for the remission of sins; but in Acts 2:38, we learn that baptism is for the remission of sins. Again, in 1 John 1:7, we are told that our Lord's blood cleanses us from sin; but in Acts 22:16, we are told that baptism cleanses us from sin. Once more, in Colossians 1:14, we are taught that Christ's blood saves us; but in 1 Peter 3:21, we are instructed that baptism saves us. How can this be? How can *both* the blood of our Lord and baptism be for the same thing—namely, the remission of our sins?

The answer is relatively simple. Our Lord's blood was shed in His death,[33] and Romans 6:3 informs us that we are baptized into His death. Therefore, it is in baptism that one first comes into contact with the precious blood of our Lord and Savior, Jesus Christ. Not literally, of course, but it is by this means that one comes into a saved relationship with the Father, Son, and Holy Spirit (Matthew 28:19). In other words, baptism is the *place* where God has agreed to save us. As Paul said in Galatians 3:27 and Romans 6:3, we are "baptized into Christ," and it is "in Christ" that all spiritual blessings reside, according to Ephesians 1:3. Such clear Bible teaching is not hard to understand but, unfortunately, multitudes have failed to comprehend it.

---

[32] See 1 John 5:8.
[33] See John 19:34.

In John 16:13, we are told that the Holy Spirit would guide the apostles into all truth. He did exactly that and, in doing so, taught that Christ's blood was shed that we might have the remission of our sins. Furthermore, He revealed that by *believing* in Christ, *repenting* of our sins, *confessing* Jesus as Lord, and *being baptized* in water by the authority of Christ, we could be saved (i.e., have our sins remitted). In other words, the "one Spirit" (namely, the Holy Spirit) has directed us to be immersed by the "one baptism" into the "one body" (i.e., the church belonging to Christ) where there is a continued cleansing provided by the blood of Christ.[34]

The Spirit, The Water, And The Blood

In 1 John 5:8, the Bible says, "And there are three that bear witness in earth: the Spirit, and the water, and the blood; and these three agree in one." In other words, the Holy Spirit, who revealed all truth, said that water baptism connects us with the saving power of Jesus' blood—blood shed for us on that cruel cross of Calvary some two thousand years ago. Therefore, if it is not in baptism that the Holy Spirit, the water, and the blood of Christ agree, then where?

In Acts 2:40, it is said that, "And with many other words he [the apostle Peter] testified and exhorted them, saying, 'Be saved from this perverse generation.'" Those who "gladly received his word [that day] were baptized" (v. 41), and the Lord added them to His church (v. 47). So, if you're not a member of the "My church" of Matthew 16:18, namely, the church—or body—of Christ, then why don't you "Repent, and be baptized...in the name of Jesus Christ for the remission of sins" (Acts 2:38)?

---

34 See Ephesians 4:4, 5; 1 Corinthians 12:13; 1 John 1:7-9.

Chapter 14

Conclusion

In concluding this study, I would like to quote once more the words of the Calvinists themselves. Commenting on the dark picture painted by the doctrine of Total Depravity, Boettner wrote: "This side of the picture is dark, very dark indeed; but its supplement is the glory of God in redemption. Each of these truths must be seen in its true light before the other can be adequately appreciated."[1] Like Boettner and his Calvinist cohorts, I accept what the Bible says about the glory of God in redemption. Indeed, the eternal God is my refuge, and underneath are the everlasting arms,[2] but I totally reject the very dark picture of the crowning glory of God's creation totally unable to positively respond to Him with love and obedience. And what does this dark picture say about Calvin's God? Where is the glory in a God who must, by the constraint of His sovereign will, coerce love and obedience from those under His care? In truth, Calvin's God is nothing more than an ogre, a being of the most brutish sort, taking by force that which has not been freely given to Him. In other words, Calvinists' God is a tyrant, and I want nothing to do with any such concept or construct.

Is the Calvinist conception anything like the picture painted of either God or man in the book of Job? Listen to and learn from the conversation between God and Satan:

---

1 Boettner, *op. cit.*, page 80.

2 Deuteronomy 33:27.

> *Then the Lord said to Satan, "Have you considered My servant Job, that there is none like him on the earth, a blameless and upright man, one who fears God and shuns evil?" So Satan answered the Lord and said, "Does Job fear God for nothing? Have You not made a hedge around him, around his household, and around all that he has on every side? You have blessed the work of his hands, and his possessions have increased in the land. But now, stretch out Your hand and touch all that he has, and he will surely curse You to Your face!" [And the Lord said to Satan, "What a complete simpleton you are Satan. Do you not know of my Eternal Decree? Job serves Me because He has no other choice. Even if he had free will, and he doesn't, he could not curse Me even if He wanted to, and all this because of My Sovereign Will and not because of anything in Job."]*[3]

No, this is *not* what God said! What He said was:

> *"Behold, all that he has is in your power; only do not lay a hand on his person." So Satan went out from the presence of the Lord.*

Of course, the lesson from Job is this: a man, of his own free will, will serve God and, in general, remain faithful to Him even when he cannot understand why God is permitting terrible things to happen to him. Job was God's servant, and he served Him because he wanted to, not because God had shackled his will and coerced him. In other words, he served God with his own free will. He could have cursed God, and there were those who urged him to do so, but he did not, and this was not because he could not, even if he wanted to, because of God's Eternal Decree. No, he continued to serve God willingly even when it looked like God had become

---

3 Job 1:8-12.

his own worst enemy. Now, what was the lesson Satan learned in all this? Was it that Job would continue to serve God because He had decreed that he would, or was it that a man would willingly continue to serve God even if all seems for naught?

Calvin was wrong, and all who espouse his doctrine are wrong. The God they serve is not the One who has revealed Himself in the Bible. They have bowed themselves down to an idol of their own making—an idol they have created for their own destruction.[4] Ironically, and the Devil loves irony, Calvinists, who think they cannot be lost, will, if they do not turn from their false system, be cut off (i.e., eternally lost) as a result of their allegiance to a false religious system, a system that, at its core, impugns both God and man.

It is my prayer that this book will help you help Calvinists see the error of their system and that, as you do so, you will not let the Calvinists define the terms we find taught in the Bible. And finally, for those of you who have never imbibed Calvinism, it is my desire that what you've learned here will assist you in keeping yourselves from idols.[5]

---

4 See Hosea 8:4.

5 1 John 5:21.

Index

Other Books By Allan Turner

The Christian & War (ISBN: 0-9777350-0-1)
The Christian & War E-book (ISBN: 0-9777350-1-X)
The Christian & Idolatry (ISBN: 0-9777350-2-8)

Allan Turner's Personal Web Site

www.allanturner.com

ALLANITA PRESS PUBLISHING

www.allanitapress.com

www.ingramcontent.com/pod-product-compliance
Lightning Source LLC
LaVergne TN
LVHW090940080826
845145LV00003B/832